Critical Thinking and

Edited by
Mark Mason

Blackwell
Publishing

Chapters © 2008 by the Authors
Book Compilation © 2008 Philosophy of Education Society of Australasia

BLACKWELL PUBLISHING
350 Main Street, Malden, MA 02148-5020, USA
9600 Garsington Road, Oxford OX4 2DQ, UK
550 Swanston Street, Carlton, Victoria 3053, Australia

First published 2008 by Blackwell Publishing Ltd

1   2008

Library of Congress Cataloging-in-Publication Data

Critical thinking and learning/edited by Mark Mason.
    p. cm.
Includes bibliographical references and index.
ISBN 978-1-4051-8107-5 (pbk.: alk. paper)
1. Critical thinking—Study and teaching.
2. Reflective learning. I. Mason, Mark.

LB1590.3.C7348 2008
370.15′2—dc22
2008003437

A catalogue record for this title is available from the British Library.

Set in 10 pt Plantin
by Graphicraft Limited, Hong Kong
Printed and bound in Singapore
by Fabulous Printers Pte Ltd

The publisher's policy is to use permanent paper from mills that operate a sustainable forestry policy, and which has been manufactured from pulp processed using acid-free and elementary chlorine-free practices. Furthermore, the publisher ensures that the text paper and cover board used have met acceptable environmental accreditation standards.

For further information on
Blackwell Publishing, visit our website at
www.blackwellpublishing.com

Contents

Notes on Contributors

Ho Mun Chan is Associate Professor of Philosophy in the Department of Public and Social Administration at the City University of Hong Kong. He graduated from the University of Hong Kong with a BA and an MPhil in Philosophy, from the University of Sussex with an MSc in Knowledge-Based Systems, and received his PhD (Philosophy and Cognitive Science) from the University of Minnesota. His research interests include ethics, social and political philosophy, and cognitive science. His recent publications include (2005) 'Rawls's Theory of Justice: A naturalistic evaluation', *Journal of Medicine and Philosophy*, 30:5, pp. 449–465, and (2004) 'Sharing Death and Dying: Advance directives, autonomy and the family', *Bioethics*, 18:2, pp. 87–103. He was granted a Full Research Excellence Award by his department in recognition of his research output in 2005–06.

Christine Doddington is Senior Lecturer in Education in the Faculty of Education at the University of Cambridge. Her interest in the education of pupils aged 3–13 is broad and is largely based within the discipline of philosophy of education. Her curriculum area of expertise is focused on drama and English. She directed the primary wing of the Nuffield funded project, 'Improving Learning: The Pupil's Agenda', and was Director of the Ofsted funded research project, 'Sustaining Pupils' Progress at Year 3'. She is reviews editor of the journal, *Education 3–13*, and as a member of the editorial team, has also edited a number of editions of the journal. She is currently Associate Director of 'The Primary Review', which is the most comprehensive review of Primary Education in England since the Plowden Report of 1967. She is co-author, with Mary Hilton, of a new book, (2007) *Child-centred Education: Reviving the creative tradition* (Thousand Oaks, CA, Sage).

Colin W. Evers is Professor of Education at the University of Hong Kong. He studied mathematics, philosophy and education before taking his PhD in philosophy of education at the University of Sydney. His teaching and research interests are in educational theory, research methodology and administrative theory. He has co-edited and co-authored six books on educational administration, including *Knowing Educational Administration*, *Exploring Educational Administration* and *Doing Educational Administration* (written with Gabriele Lakomski), and some eighty papers in his areas of research interest.

Duck-Joo Kwak is Assistant Professor at Konkuk University in Seoul, Korea. As co-editor of *Korean Philosophy of Education*, her research interests are in ethics, philosophy of education, and teacher education. She has published numerous articles on civic and moral education, especially in relation to democratic citizenship in liberal Confucian culture. Her current work also focuses on practical wisdom in teaching for teacher education.

Chi-Ming Lam is a PhD candidate in philosophy of education in the Faculty of Education at the University of Hong Kong. His research interests include the philosophy of Karl Popper, critical thinking, and philosophy for children. He has published articles on critical thinking and philosophy for children in *New Horizons in Education* and in *Thinking: The Journal of Philosophy for Children*. He is currently researching how to promote critical thinking in children through Matthew Lipman's Philosophy for Children programme.

Kam Louie is Professor and Dean of the Arts Faculty at the University of Hong Kong. He has over ten books under his name, including (2002) *Theorising Chinese Masculinity* (Cambridge University Press) and (1997, with Bonnie McDougall) *The Literature of China in the Twentieth Century* (New York, Columbia University Press). He is editor of *Asian Studies Review* and a Fellow of the Australian Academy of Humanities. He is currently editing the *Cambridge Handbook of Modern Chinese Culture* and researching Chinese diasporic literature and how Chinese masculinity is altered as it travels to the West.

Michael Luntley is Professor and Head of the Department of Philosophy at the University of Warwick. His main research interests are Wittgenstein, the metaphysics of thought and reasons, and perceptual knowledge, especially the role perceptually dependent knowledge bases play in expert performance. One of the central themes of his book (2003) *Wittgenstein: Meaning and judgement* (Oxford, Blackwell), is the idea that competence with language consists in seeing things aright, rather than being in possession of knowledge subject to a theoretical articulation. This work underpins some of his interests in the metaphysics of reasons, including particularism about reasons. In the philosophy of education he is especially interested in the nature of professional expertise. He is currently investigating the scope for a detailed account of epistemic virtues—detailed cognitive skills by which experts of various kinds manage the complex environments with which they deal. He was recently director of the research project, 'Attention and the Knowledge Bases of Expertise', funded by an AHRB Innovation Award. The project involved a pilot study of the cognitive skills that underpin the competences of class teachers.

Mark Mason is Associate Professor in Philosophy and Educational Studies in the Faculty of Education at the University of Hong Kong, where he is also Director of the Comparative Education Research Centre (CERC). With research interests in philosophy, educational studies, comparative education and educational development, he is Regional Editor (Asia & The Pacific) of the *International Journal of Educational Development*, Editor of the CERC *Studies in Comparative Education Series* (co-published by Springer), and President of the Comparative Education Society of Hong Kong. His philosophical research interest in critical reasoning led to his appointment as Programme Chair of the 34th Annual PESA Conference ('Critical Thinking and Learning: Values, concepts and issues'), one outcome of which is this special issue.

Michael A. Peters is Professor of Education at the University of Illinois at Urbana-Champaign. He is the Executive Editor of *Educational Philosophy and Theory*, and Editor of two electronic journals, *Policy Futures in Education* and *E-Learning*. His research interests are in education, philosophy and social policy, and he has written over two hundred articles and chapters and some thirty books, including most recently *Why Foucault? New Directions in Educational Research* (Peter Lang,

2007), *Building Knowledge Cultures: Education and Development in the Age of Knowledge Capitalism* (Rowman & Littlefield, 2006), both with Tina (A. C.) Besley, and *Knowledge Economy, Development and the Future of the University* (Sense, 2007).

Janette Ryan is Senior Lecturer in Pedagogy and Curriculum in the Faculty of Education at Monash University, Australia. She is the author of *A Guide to Teaching International Students* (Oxford Centre for Staff and Learning Development, 2000) and co-editor of *Teaching International Students: Improving Learning for All* (Routledge, 2005). Her research interests include the social and cultural aspects of pedagogy and curriculum. She has taught or studied in a range of Anglophone schools and universities, as well as in China. She is currently researching China's educational reform in a collaborative project with Chinese, Australian and Canadian academics and teachers.

Hektor K. T. Yan is an Instructor in the Department of Public and Social Administration at the City University of Hong Kong. His research interests include ethics and comparative philosophy. Formerly he worked as a Research Fellow for the Teaching Development Grant Project, 'Enhancing Moral Reasoning and Moral Imagination in Ethics Education'. With Julia Tao, he co-edited *Meaning of Life* (McGraw-Hill Education, 2006), a philosophy textbook specifically designed for Hong Kong undergraduates and non-specialists.

Preface and acknowledgements

This volume in the Blackwell *Educational Philosophy and Theory* Monograph Series is based on a special issue that marked a first both for the journal and for the Philosophy of Education Society of Australasia (PESA). As was the case with the special issue, this monograph is comprised of a selection of papers presented at PESA's 34th Annual Conference, held at the Hong Kong Institute of Education in November 2005.

The fact that we have been able to devote an entire issue to the conference is possible because of the high quality of papers presented. The conference theme, 'Critical Thinking and Learning: Values, concepts and issues', reflected in the title of the monograph and the special issue, invited consideration of these and related debates. Many colleagues in the field responded by submitting papers related to these themes, and the plenary sessions of the conference were focused on these questions. As such, it made for a tremendously successful conference—many said one of PESA's best, not only in terms of the high rate of participation (remarkably, at the first PESA conference ever held outside of Australia and New Zealand), but also because of the focused plenary sessions made for a conversation that continued through the conference.

Mark Mason chaired the Programme Committee, and it is in that capacity that he has edited the special issue and the monograph. My thanks are due to him, to the members of the Programme Committee (Derek Sankey, Chi-Ming Lam and Kenny Huen), to those keynote and plenary speakers who assisted in the selection of papers for publication, and to the authors themselves, for a very fine special issue and monograph. Collections of papers selected from those presented at a conference can vary in quality. This selection ranks with the best of them, not only because of the quality of the papers, but also because of the thematic coherence and theoretical integrity of the volume as a whole. Questions which are central to the theme of critical thinking and learning are explored here in some detail, with a high degree of philosophical sophistication, and in a manner in which papers respond to each other, differing with and complementing each other—as they did in the conference.

One conference paper is missing from this selection—that of the third keynote speaker, Harvey Siegel. Harvey's paper, 'Multiculturalism and Rationality', was already committed elsewhere, and could not be included here. It continued a conversation among the three keynote speakers that ultimately revolved around the question of rationality across cultures. However, as Mark Mason notes, the coherence and theoretical integrity of this special issue are, fortunately, not too compromised by the absence of this paper, for Colin Evers picks up a similar theme in his paper and defends a conclusion that is consistent with Siegel's and that contrasts with that of my own.

As Executive Editor of *Educational Philosophy and Theory* I would like to acknowledge the Conference Organiser, Derek Sankey, the Conference Secretary, Yan Chan, and their team at the Hong Kong Institute of Education for a most successful conference, one outcome of which is this monograph that contributes original material and new thought to educational questions of tremendous importance, offering different theoretical conceptions and going to the heart of contemporary debates about thinking, learning styles, curriculum, cultural difference, citizenship, and the knowledge economy. Finally, I would like to acknowledge the expert editorial skills of Mark Mason, who not only chaired the Conference Programme Committee, but also edited the special issue and this monograph.

MICHAEL A. PETERS
University of Illinois at Urbana-Champaign

1
Critical Thinking and Learning

MARK MASON
Faculty of Education, The University of Hong Kong

The goals of 'critical thinking' and of 'life-long' and 'life-wide learning' appear frequently in the rhetoric of current educational reform in many societies across the globe. What are the discourses that produce these educational aims, and what are the values associated with these discourses? What do these concepts mean, and what societal, cultural and educational issues arise from them? How are critical thinking and learning related? They appear to enjoy a largely unquestioned co-existence in the contemporary educational literature, much of which concludes that if students are to learn to think, they should be encouraged to ask critical questions. Teachers, we read, should employ classroom strategies that produce active rather than passive learners, given the demands of 'the global economy', which apparently needs active, creative, and critical workers who are 'life-long' and 'life-wide' learners.

This special issue of *Educational Philosophy and Theory*, constituted by a selection of papers presented at the 34th Annual Conference of the Philosophy of Education Society of Australasia, held at the Hong Kong Institute of Education in November 2005, invited critical consideration of these and related issues. Education in the different countries of Australasia and Asia is informed by widely differing historical and cultural perspectives, from western to Confucian, from liberal to communitarian, from colonial to postcolonial. Hong Kong, in many ways, lies at the crossroads of many of these perspectives. To what extent, for example, are the dominant concepts of thinking and learning a product of 'western' cultural values? Might they be in conflict with concepts and values said to be prevalent in many Confucian-heritage cultures that apparently stress the meditative mind, harmony of thought and harmony in relationships, filial piety, a tempered questioning of authority, and the transmission of received wisdom through time? Might the liberal ideal of the independent and autonomous individual clash with communitarian values of identity in relationship? What are the consequences for communitarian education in the Islamic societies of Australasia and Asia? How might one reconcile the phenomenon, well documented among many Asian students, of learning by induction from rote memorization—the 'paradox of Asian learners'—with western ideals of learning and of the growth of knowledge by critical questioning? According to Popper, after all, one learns little by simply rehearsing what is already known: new knowledge develops by critically falsifying the known.

In the following section I offer a brief sketch of some of the different perspectives in the field of critical thinking, for the chief purposes of highlighting the differences among them and of setting the ground on which subsequent debates in this issue take place. Once the broad contours of some of the debates in the field are thus established, it becomes clear that numerous questions arise. Does rationality transcend particular cultures, or are there different kinds of thinking, different styles of reasoning? What is the relationship between critical thinking and learning? In what ways does the moral domain overlap with these largely epistemic and pedagogical issues? The final section of the paper introduces the other papers in this collection, showing how they, separately and in groups, respond to these questions.

What is Critical Thinking?

My intention here is briefly to highlight the apparent differences between some of the better-known positions in the field. To this end, different philosophers who have developed theories of critical thinking are considered. Some argue that critical thinking is constituted by particular skills, such as the ability to assess reasons properly, or to weigh relevant evidence, or to identify fallacious arguments. Others argue that it is most importantly a critical attitude or disposition, such as the tendency to ask probing questions, or a critical orientation, or some such attribute intrinsic to character. Or, if critical thinking is constituted by dispositional knowledge, some suggest that this would be in the sense of a moral perspective or set of values that motivates critical thinking. Still others argue that it is constituted by substantial knowledge of particular content. Some mean by this, knowledge about concepts in critical thinking such as premises, assumptions, or valid arguments. And others mean deep and wide knowledge of a particular discipline and its epistemological structure, so that one is a critical thinker only within that discipline.

Five philosophers of education who defend one or another of these positions, and whom, among others, I consider briefly here for the purpose of establishing the parameters of the debate, are Robert Ennis, Richard Paul, John McPeck, Harvey Siegel, and Jane Roland Martin. Ennis defends a conception of critical thinking based primarily in particular skills; Paul also emphasizes the skills associated with critical thinking. McPeck argues that critical thinking is specific to a particular discipline, and that it depends on a thorough knowledge and understanding of the content and epistemology of the discipline. Siegel, for whom critical thinking means to be 'appropriately moved by reasons', defends both a 'reason assessment component' in the skills domain, and a 'critical attitude component' in the dispositional domain. Martin, who emphasizes the dispositions associated with critical thinking, suggests that it is motivated by and founded in moral perspectives and particular values. More recent contributions to the field, such as those by Barbara Thayer-Bacon, Kal Alston and Anne Phelan, have tended to push the boundaries of the domain opened up by Martin in this regard.

Ennis (1996) defends a conception of critical thinking based primarily in particular skills, such as observing, inferring, generalizing, reasoning, evaluating reasoning, and the like. For him, critical thinking is 'the correct assessing of statements', but he has also defined it more generally as 'reasonable reflective thinking'. Ennis (1992) maintains that the skills associated with critical thinking can be learned independently of specific disciplines, and can be transferred from one domain to another. He does, however, acknowledge that a certain minimum competence in a particular discipline is essential before one can apply the skills of critical thought to that domain. For him, the process of critical thinking is deductive: it involves applying the principles and skills of critical thought to a particular discipline. In response to criticism that his conception of critical thinking focuses only on skills, Ennis has more recently included in his definition a notion of a tendency to think critically.

Like Ennis, Paul (1982) emphasizes the skills and processes associated with critical thinking. He distinguishes critical thinking in the weak sense from critical thinking in the strong sense. In the weak sense it implies the ability to think critically about positions other than one's own; and in the strong sense, the ability to think critically about one's own position, arguments, assumptions, and world-view as well. For Paul, critical thinking includes a deep knowledge of oneself, which takes both intellectual courage and humility. A strong critical thinker is able to understand the bigger picture holistically, to see different worldviews in perspective, rather than just to critique the individual steps in a particular argument. For him, dialogue with others who are different, who have different worldviews and cultural backgrounds, is an essential feature of critical thinking. We thus learn to see things from different perspectives, to contextualize our worldview within the bigger picture.[1] A positive consequence is the tolerance we may learn as a result. For Paul then, critical thinking is thinking aimed at overcoming 'egocentric and sociocentric thinking'. Siegel takes issue with Paul here, suggesting that this tolerance may be merely a tolerance born in relativism. Siegel fears a descent into relativism, and demands an epistemological anchor for critical thinking, core reasons that are open to public scrutiny and understanding.

Unlike Ennis and Paul, McPeck (1981) argues that critical thinking is specific to a particular discipline, and that it depends on a thorough knowledge and understanding of the content and epistemology of the discipline. For him, critical thinking cannot be taught independently of a particular subject domain. His point is that it's difficult to be a critical thinker in the domain of nuclear physics if one knows very little about it. No matter what critical thinking skills and dispositions one might have, wide and deep knowledge of a discipline is essential for critical thought in that domain. This means that critical thinking implies a thorough knowledge of the discipline in which one is working, of its content and its epistemology: what constitute the truth of premises and the validity of argument in that discipline, how one would apply them, what the criteria are for the use of technical language in the field in argumentation, and the like. For McPeck, the process of critical thinking is inductive: it involves inducing the principles of critical thought by generalization from the content and structure of the discipline.

Siegel stresses a strong conceptual connection between critical thinking and rationality. For him, critical thinking means to be 'appropriately moved by reasons', and to be rational is to 'believe and act on the basis of reasons'. As did Peters and Scheffler before him, Siegel points out that to accept the importance and force of reasons is to commit oneself to abide consistently by publicly defensible principles that are accepted as universal and objective. For Scheffler, principles, reasons and consistency are conceptually inextricable. In these terms, critical thinking is principled thinking, at least in terms of the principles of impartiality, consistency, non-arbitrariness and fairness. We will see that Martin develops further the idea of critical thinking being based on principles, but in a different sense—primarily the principle of justice.

Siegel's conception of critical thinking defends both a 'reason assessment component' in the skills domain, and a 'critical attitude component' in the dispositional domain. With respect to the 'reason assessment component',

> [t]he critical thinker must be able to assess reasons and their ability to warrant beliefs, claims and actions properly. Therefore, the critical thinker must have a good understanding of, and the ability to utilize, both subject-specific and subject-neutral (logical) principles governing the assessment of reasons. (Siegel, 1990, p. 38)

We have seen that Ennis emphasizes the principles and skills of critical reasoning that are subject-neutral, that is, the principles of logic which are not particular to any one discipline, but universally applicable. On the other hand, McPeck emphasizes the importance of subject-specific principles and skills, that is, the principles that apply only to a particular discipline, such as those that apply in aesthetics to the proper assessment of art. Siegel makes short work of this longstanding disagreement between them, pointing out that both subject-neutral and subject-specific principles and skills are relevant to reason assessment and hence to critical thinking. More than these two domains of principles and skills, Siegel asserts that a further essential aspect of critical thinking entails a deeper epistemological understanding of 'the nature of reasons, warrant, and justification'. In other words, a critical thinker needs to understand why 'a given putative reason is to be assessed' as such.

With respect to Siegel's 'critical attitude component',

> [o]ne who has the critical attitude has a certain character as well as certain skills: a character which is inclined to seek, and to base judgment and action upon, reasons; which rejects partiality and arbitrariness; which is committed to the objective evaluation of relevant evidence; and which values such aspects of critical thinking as intellectual honesty, justice to evidence, sympathetic and impartial consideration of interests, objectivity, and impartiality. (Siegel, 1990, p. 39)

This position endorses strongly that a love of reason and a commitment to give expression to the principles and skills of critical reasoning are essential attributes of the critical thinker.

Martin (1992) emphasizes the dispositions associated with critical thinking, and suggests that it is motivated by and founded in moral perspectives and particular values. Starting from a question about the purpose of critical thinking, she suggests that it should be motivated by a concern for a more humane and just world. Just because someone may reach a conclusion by some brilliant critical reasoning, it doesn't follow that his conclusion is morally acceptable. For Martin, the purpose of critical thinking is morally grounded. In contrast to Siegel's epistemological anchor for critical thinking, she suggests that it needs a moral anchor. In fact, for Martin the issue of critical thinking is not the primary issue. Most important for her are thinking and engagement with others that are oriented towards the development of a better world. Thayer-Bacon breaks further the ground opened by Martin in her defence of 'the value of embracing pluralistic and democratic commitments on epistemological grounds as well as moral grounds' (2001, p. 23) in the transformation of critical thinking to what she calls 'constructive thinking' (ibid., p. 5). Defending similarly a notion of critical thinking, which she calls 'connective criticism' (Alston, 2001, p. 28), that is engaged with the world, Alston suggests that critical thinkers will, in this account, 'be attuned to the varieties of human problems ... [and] will be able to envision ways of making meaningful connections between thought, activity, expression, and relationship' (ibid., p. 38). Phelan, similarly situated in what Walters (1994, p. 18) calls 'second wave critical thinking', continues in this vein with her idea of 'practical wisdom as an alternative to current formulations of critical thinking' (Phelan, 2001, p. 41) that rely, in Walters's description of 'first wave' critical thinking, solely on 'the canons of logical analysis and argumentation' (Walters, 1994, p. 4). For Phelan, critical thinking that relies solely on reason is limited in its ability to respond to the realm of the practical—'the death of a child; a sick patient; ... political conflict; an adolescent's resistance' (2001, p. 42). Practical wisdom recognizes that 'how we are to respond on any of these occasions may be more than an epistemological question' (ibid.).

Each of the philosophers I've considered here emphasizes a particular feature that he or she defends as the most important aspect of critical thinking. Each tends to emphasize one, perhaps two, of the following:

- The skills of critical reasoning (such as the ability to assess reasons properly);
- A disposition, in the sense of:
  - A critical attitude (scepticism, the tendency to ask probing questions) and the commitment to give expression to this attitude, or
  - A moral orientation which motivates critical thinking;
- Substantial knowledge of particular content, whether of:
  - Concepts in critical thinking (such as necessary and sufficient conditions), or of
  - A particular discipline, in which one is then capable of critical thought.

Most debates around critical thinking tend to stress at least the skills and dispositions associated with a sceptical, reasonable, and reflective approach. Ennis and Paul, as we have seen, emphasize the skills component of critical thinking most strongly; and Siegel's 'reason assessment component' of critical thinking emphasizes the ability to assess reasons properly. The disposition to think critically is emphasized to a varying degree by each: Ennis points to the importance of a 'tendency' to think critically; Paul points to the importance of a critical disposition being 'intrinsic to the character of a person'; Siegel stresses a critical attitude as the second of his two components of critical thinking; McPeck speaks of the 'disposition' or 'propensity' to think critically. The emphasis in the dispositional domain of Martin, Thayer-Bacon, Alston, and Phelan is different. Their stress, speaking very generally, is on a moral foundation of humane compassion and commitment to justice that motivates, informs, and constitutes the goal of critical thinking. McPeck emphasizes most strongly the need to have substantial knowledge of a particular discipline before one can be capable of critical reasoning in that domain. Ennis, however, emphasizes most strongly, albeit in an implicit manner, the importance of knowledge of the concepts associated with critical thought. It may be that an integrated conception of critical thinking, such as I have discussed elsewhere (see Mason, 2000), would need to be constituted by all five of these components: the skills of critical reasoning; a critical attitude; a moral orientation; knowledge of the concepts of critical reasoning; and knowledge of a particular discipline. If these are indeed the necessary conditions for integrated critical thinking, then what I mean by this term is thinking that is of course not entrenched in dogma (although committed to reason), is willing to consider multiple perspectives, is informed, sceptical, and entails sound reasoning.

Critical Thinking and Learning

Having established the contours of some of the debates in the field of critical thinking, numerous questions arise. Does rationality transcend particular cultures, or are there different kinds of thinking, different styles of reasoning? Are there, for example, 'East-West' differences in reasoning styles? If not, what might be the justificatory conditions for a trans-cultural conception of rationality? Four papers in this issue address these questions: those by Michael Peters; Colin Evers; Ho Mun Chan and Hektor Yan; and Janette Ryan and Kam Louie.

A second group of questions has to do with some specifics of the relationship between critical thinking and learning. Is there a distinction between learning activities that involve training and those that involve reasoning? How might we teach for the development of critical thinking? Is Popper's falsificationist heuristic, for example, a helpful resource for developing critical thinking? Two authors address these questions in their papers: Michael Luntley, and Chi-Ming Lam.

A third group of questions introduces the moral domain more substantially into these largely epistemic and pedagogical considerations. Should the capacity for rational and critical thought be viewed as the prime justification for treating persons with respect? How might the teaching of critical thinking in moral education help young people to avoid moral relativism yet respond coherently to cultural pluralism? The last two papers in this collection, those by Christine Doddington and by Duck-Joo Kwak, respond to these questions.

In response to the contemporary tendency 'to treat thinking ahistorically and aculturally as though physiology, brain structure and human evolution are all there is to say about thinking which is worthwhile or educationally significant', Michael

Peters offers a historical and 'pluralized' philosophical picture of thinking. In his paper, 'Kinds of Thinking, Styles of Reasoning', he challenges the dominant focus on universal processes of logic and reasoning in the field of critical thinking by drawing on Nietzsche, Heidegger, Wittgenstein, Critical Theory and French post-structuralist philosophy, in defence of different kinds of thinking and styles of reasoning. His interpretation and argument establish the importance of philosophical and historical accounts of thinking and reasoning: he presents these accounts as radically historical and pluralist. As he concludes, they introduce theoretical contestability into accounts of thinking that take us away from the pure realms of cognitive science and logic and towards views that are historical, temporal, spatial, cultural, and therefore empirical.

It has already been noted in the Foreword introducing this special issue that Harvey Siegel's paper, 'Multiculturalism and Rationality', presented as a keynote address at the conference, is missing from this collection because it had already been committed to another publication. However, it is worth noting a key question that Siegel asks in his paper: is rationality culture-specific? The question continues the themes raised by Michael Peters in his paper. While Peters, as just noted, concludes that we should understand thinking in at least historical and cultural context, Siegel argues that, while different cultures do indeed differ in their evaluations of the rational status of particular arguments, 'rationality itself' is best understood as transcending particular cultures. The coherence and theoretical integrity of this special issue are, fortunately, not too compromised by the absence of Siegel's paper, for Colin Evers picks up a similar theme in his paper and defends a conclusion that is consistent with Siegel's.

In his paper, 'Culture, Cognitive Pluralism and Rationality', written in response to several empirical studies that apparently show systematic culture-based differences in patterns of reasoning, Evers defends the possibility of objectivity in reasoning strategies across cultures. He argues that there is at least one class of exceptions to the claim that there are alternative, culture-specific and equally warranted standards of good reasoning: the class that entails the solution of certain well-structured problems which, suitably chosen, are common, or touchstone, to the sorts of culturally different viewpoints discussed. He argues and provides evidence that some cognitive tasks are seen in much the same way across cultures, not least by virtue of the common run of experiences with the world of material objects in early childhood by creatures with similar cognitive endowments. These tasks thus present as similarly structured sets of claims that have similar priority: what is framed, and what is bracketed, or held constant in the background, he shows to be naturally common across cultures. As a consequence, Evers concludes, a normative view of reasoning and, by implication, critical thinking can be defended. More than providing some justificatory conditions for transcultural rationality, he suggests that, while this might be a modest sense of objectivity, the high level of intercultural articulation that is able to occur among people of different backgrounds indicates that it provides cognitive scaffolding for many other reasoning tasks as well.

In their paper, 'Is There a Geography of Thought for East-West Differences? Why or why not?', Ho Mun Chan and Hektor Yan challenge, as does Evers, Richard

Nisbett's claims as to 'how Asians and Westerners think differently' in his book, *The Geography of Thought* (2003). Chan and Yan argue that Nisbett's claimed differences between Asian and Western thinking styles are either not real or at best overstated. This they do by outlining a naturalistic approach to the study of human rationality, developing from it the notions of ideal rationality, adaptive rationality and critical rationality, and thence constructing a geography of thinking styles that is different to Nisbett's. Thus they reject Nisbett's claim that East Asians have a stronger tendency to think 'illogically' than do Westerners. They do, however, echo Michael Peters's conclusions by agreeing with Nisbett that reasoning (or critical thinking) is not a homogeneous phenomenon, and that there are different ways or forms of reasoning. For Chan and Yan they are often adaptive strategies in response to particular problems in human life. Among the implications for teaching critical thinking are that students should be taught to be more aware of the natural and cultural contexts in which their thinking styles are embedded, so that they might become more sensitive to their own ways of thinking and thus less likely to misapply them or make hasty judgements based on them.

Janette Ryan and Kam Louie continue in the same vein as Chan and Yan. In their paper, 'False Dichotomy? "Western" and "Eastern" Concepts of Scholarship and Learning', they offer strong cautions with regard to prevailing stereotyped views of 'Western' and 'Eastern' learners. Ryan and Louie remind us how students from Confucian-heritage cultures are often characterised as 'passive, dependent, surface/ rote learners prone to plagiarism and lacking critical thinking', while students from 'Western' cultures are characterised as 'assertive and independent, critical thinkers'. Such binary classifications do not, suggest Ryan and Louie, take account of the complexities and diversity of educational philosophies and practices that characterize any educational milieu, 'Western', 'Eastern', or whatever else. Their paper uses the Confucian-Western dichotomy as a case study to suggest that 'attributing particular unanalysed concepts to whole systems of cultural practice leads to misunderstand-ings and bad teaching practice'. It would be good if educationists were aware of the differences and complexities within cultures before they examined and compared across cultures. This, in their view, entails a 'meta-cultural awareness' and a willingness to meet the learning needs of all students, regardless of their cultural background.

Turning to the question of some of the specific issues in the relationship between critical thinking and learning, Michael Luntley begins his paper, 'Learning, Empowerment and Judgement', with a distinction that is deeply rooted in our conceptions of learning and that is apparently simple and compelling: the distinc-tion between learning activities that involve training and those that involve reason-ing. In the first, the pupil is understood as a passive recipient of habits of mind and action, acquiring these habits by mimesis rather than by reasoning. Learning by reasoning, on the other hand, involves considerable mental activity on the part of the pupil, who, using her own capacity to reason, has to work out what to think and do. Luntley argues that there is no basis for this distinction, that learning by reasoning is the only credible form of learning. He defends this thesis both by reviewing the empirical evidence from developmental psychology for a rationalist account of language learning as learning by reasoning, and by providing a philo-sophical argument against learning as training and in favour of a rationalist model of learning by reasoning. He shows that, in line with the empirical data regarding first language learning, there is no such thing as learning by training. In a careful reading of Wittgenstein's account of the learning of words, he shows that although Wittgenstein appears to endorse, at the most basic level of language acquisition, the idea of learning by training, it makes more sense to read him as endorsing an account of learning by reasoning. This account of learning, claims Luntley, requires a rethinking of the activity central to learning; a rethinking that requires, in turn, a rethinking of the subject, the agent whose most basic activity is the mental activity of reasoning. Further, acknowledging the centrality of reasoning in learning means empowering the learner by acknowledging her as 'an active reasoner, a judge, not a mimic, someone who in response to the teacher's invitation to join in the business of reasoning and making sense of ourselves, does so with autonomy'.

Chi-Ming Lam gets down to some specific and pertinent issues in the teaching of critical thinking in his 'Is Popper's Falsificationist Heuristic a Helpful Resource for Developing Critical Thinking?'. In Popper's falsificationist epistemology know-ledge grows through conjectural refutation—criticizing and falsifying existing theories. Since criticism plays such an important role in his methodology, Lam asks the obvious question: is Popper's heuristic a helpful resource for developing critical thinking? He finds much controversy in the psychological literature over the feasi-bility and utility of Popper's falsificationism as a heuristic. Considering Popper's falsificationism within the framework of his critical rationalism, and elucidating the interrelated concepts of fallibilism, criticism, and verisimilitude, Lam concludes that the implementation of this heuristic means exposing to criticism various philosophical presuppositions that work against criticism itself, including the doctrine that truth is manifest, the demand for precision in concepts as a prerequisite for criticism, essentialism, instrumentalism, and conventionalism; it also means combating the confirmation bias (to which Popper did not pay much attention) through such educational means as helping teachers and students to acquire an awareness of its pervasiveness and various guises, teaching them to think of several alternative hypotheses simultaneously in seeking explanation of phenomena, encouraging them to assess evidence objectively in the formation and evaluation of hypotheses, and cultivating in them an appropriate attitude towards inconsistent data. With regard to the feasibility of teaching students to falsify, Lam concludes that it is if teachers adopt relatively simple inference tasks while creating an opportunity for students to collaborate with each other and lowering the normativity of the learning envi-ronment. With respect to whether teachers *should* teach students to falsify, Lam finds that although disconfirmation might be an effective heuristic when students cannot appeal to an outside authority to test their hypotheses, it appears not to be a universally effective strategy for solving reasoning problems. In contrast, con-firmation seems not to be completely counterproductive and might be a useful heuristic, especially in the early stages of generating hypotheses. Whether dis-confirmation or confirmation is better often depends on the characteristics of the specific task at hand.

Christine Doddington reminds us that critical thinking has come to be defined as and aligned with 'good' thinking. This conception reflects the value we place on rationality, and is woven into our ideas of what it means to become a person and hence deserving of respect. In her paper, 'Critical Thinking as a Source of Respect for Persons: A critique', she considers some challenges to this view that have implications for our understanding of what it is to become a person. The capacity for critical thought may indeed, she accepts, be one significant aspect of developed personhood; however, an emphasis on critical thought as the main source of respect for persons raises a number of issues about what might therefore be excluded or neglected. She draws on some different perspectives to retrieve what she calls a more 'humanised' view of how we exist in the world and to suggest that human consciousness as a mark of personhood should be seen as rooted in bodily senses and a more aesthetic orientation towards the world that moves us away from critical thought and rationality as the single or prime indicators of 'good' thinking. She draws the educational implication that we need a curriculum that recognizes fully the richness and primacy of sense, perception and embodied personal thinking, all of which, she claims, cannot be subsumed into what we currently understand as critical thought. What she shows, in sum, is that to educate a thinking person cannot, and should not, be just about educating him or her to think critically. In this we show respect for the whole person, and not just for the person who has developed the capacity for rationally based critical thought.

Duck-Joo Kwak follows Christine Doddington in asking questions about the relationship of the ethical to the epistemic in debates about critical thinking. In her paper, 'Re-conceptualizing Critical Thinking for Moral Education in Culturally Plural Societies', she seeks new ways of conceptualizing critical thinking for moral education in a world increasingly characterized by culturally diverse societies. This she does by examining Harvey Siegel's modernist notion of critical thinking and Nicholas Burbules's (soft) postmodern critique, seeking an answer to the question how the teaching of critical thinking in moral education can help young people to avoid moral relativism yet respond coherently to cultural pluralism. Kwak takes Bernard Williams's concept of 'ethical reflection' as a possible candidate and explores this concept as a means of accommodating these concerns.

Note

1. Paul's strong sense critical thinking offers useful assistance in overcoming reified perceptions of local arrangements. The mistaken reasoning of reification, in 'because this is the way things are, this is the way they should be', is ultimately an example of Hume's 'is to ought fallacy': it is of course questionable whether one can derive a normative conclusion from empirical premises.

References

Alston, K. (2001) Re/Thinking Critical Thinking: The seductions of everyday life, *Studies in Philosophy and Education*, 20:1.

Ennis, R. (1996) *Critical Thinking* (Upper Saddle River, NJ, Prentice-Hall).

Ennis, R. (1992) Conflicting Views on Teaching Critical Reasoning, in: R. Talaska (ed.), *Critical Reasoning in Contemporary Culture* (Albany, SUNY Press).

Martin, J. R. (1992) Critical Thinking for a Humane World, in: S. Norris (ed.), *The Generalizability of Critical Thinking: Multiple perspectives on an educational ideal* (New York, Teachers College Press).

McPeck, J. (1981) *Critical Thinking and Education* (Oxford, Martin Robertson).

Mason, M. (2000) Integrated Critical Thinking, in: T. McLaughlin (ed.), *Proceedings of the Thirty-fourth Annual Conference of the Philosophy of Education Society of Great Britain* (Oxford, Philosophy of Education Society of Great Britain).

Paul, R. (1982) Teaching Critical Thinking in the 'Strong Sense': A focus on self-deception, world views, and a dialectical mode of analysis, *Informal Logic Newsletter*, 4:2.

Phelan, A. (2001) The Death of a Child and the Birth of Practical Wisdom, *Studies in Philosophy and Education*, 20:1.

Siegel, H. (1990) *Educating Reason: Rationality, critical thinking and education* (London, Routledge).

Thayer-Bacon, B. (2001) Radical Democratic Communities Always-in-the-Making, *Studies in Philosophy and Education*, 20:1.

Walters, K. (1994) *Re-Thinking Reason: New perspectives in critical thinking* (New York, SUNY Press).

Kinds of Thinking, Styles of Reasoning

MICHAEL A. PETERS

University of Illinois at Urbana-Champaign, Universities of Glasgow and Auckland

> A *picture* held us captive.
>
> Ludwig Wittgenstein, *Philosophical Investigations*, #115.

> What is given to thinking to think is not some deeply hidden underlying meaning, but rather something lying near, that which lies nearest, which because it is only this, we have therefore always already passed over.
>
> Martin Heidegger, 'Nietzsche's Word: God is dead',
> *The Question Concerning Technology*, p. 111.

Introduction: Why the Present Emphasis on Thinking?

There is no more central issue to education than thinking. Certainly, such an emphasis chimes with the rationalist and cognitive deep structure of the Western educational tradition. The contemporary tendency reinforced by first generation cognitive psychology was to treat thinking ahistorically and aculturally as though physiology, brain structure and human evolution are all there is to say about thinking that is worthwhile or educationally significant. Harré and Gillet (1994) provide a brief account of the shift from what they call 'the Old Paradigm' of behaviourism and experimentalism, based on an outdated philosophical theory of science and metaphysics, towards psychology as a cognitive science in its first and second waves. The impetus for change from the Old Paradigm they suggest came from two sources: the 'new' social psychology which took its start from G. H. Mead and, more importantly, the 'new' cognitive psychology that developed out of the work of Bruner and G. A. Miller and P. N. Johnson-Laird. They maintain that the second cognitive revolution began under the influence of the writings of the later Wittgenstein (1953), which gave a central place to language and discourse and attempted to overcome the Cartesian picture of mental activity as a set of inner processes. The main principles of the second revolution pointed to how psychological phenomena should be treated as features of discourse, and thus as a public and social activity. Hence: 'Individual and private uses of symbolic systems, which in this view constitute thinking, are derived from interpersonal discursive processes ...' (Harré & Gillet, 1994, p. 27). The production of psychological phenomena, including emotions and attitudes, are seen to depend upon the actors' skills, their 'positionality' and the story lines they develop (Howie & Peters, 1996; Peters & Appel, 1996). The third 'revolution', also utilising Wittgenstein (among other theorists), was advanced by social psychologists such as John Shotter (e.g. 1993) and Kenneth Gergen (1985; 1991). These views also emphasized a social construction rather than an individualist cognitivist construction. Gergen (2001) acknowledges the sociology of knowledge tradition and maintains that once knowledge became denaturalised and re-enculturated the terms passed more broadly into the discourses of the human sciences.[1]

The movement of critical thinking also tends to treat thinking ahistorically, focusing on universal processes of logic and reasoning.[2] Against this trend and against the scientific spirit of the age this paper presents a historical and philosophical picture of thinking. By contrast with dominant cognitive and logical models, the paper emphasizes *kinds of thinking* and *styles of reasoning*. The paper grows out of interests primarily in the work of Nietzsche (Peters, 2000; Peters *et al.*, 2001a), Heidegger (Peters, 2002) and Wittgenstein (Peters & Marshall, 1999; Peters, 2000; 2001a,b; 2002), and in its extension and development in Critical Theory (Peters *et al.*, 2003a,b) and French poststructuralist philosophy (e.g. Peters, 2003a,b,c). The paper draws directly on some of this work to argue for the recognition of different *kinds of thinking*, which are explored by reference to Heidegger, and also the significance of *styles of reasoning*, which are explored by reference to Wittgenstein and to Ian Hacking.

I begin with the admonition, 'Always historicize! Always pluralize!', for Reason also has a history. The narrative of critical reason has at least five 'chapters' beginning, first, with Kant; followed by, second, its bifurcation with Horkheimer and Adorno into theoretical and practical reason; third, its separation into three by Habermas (1987) according to knowledge interests—technical, practical and emancipatory; and, finally, its pluralisation in the material conditions of discourses (Wittgenstein, Foucault, Lyotard). The fifth chapter is in a sense a postscript—a working out of the consequences of accepting that reason, like knowledge and the value of knowledge, is rooted in social relations. In some forms this is both a naturalisation and a pluralisation of Kant: not one reason, but many. It is clear that the history of reason is the history of philosophy itself, and as history, both revisable and open to interpretation.

To talk of 'thinking skills'—a concept that dominates contemporary educational discourse—is already to adopt a particular view of thinking, that is, thinking as a kind of technology. This view of thinking is a reductive concept of thinking as a means-ends instrumentality, a series of techniques that can move us from one space to another. In the so-called knowledge economy emphasis in the curriculum has passed from the knowledge and understanding of traditional subjects and disciplines to generic, *transferable skills* that allegedly equip learners with the means by which they can learn. These are often described in psychological language as metacognitive skills, that is, learning how to learn, and are now squared off against information-processing skills, knowledge management skills, entrepreneurial skills, and social skills like team-building.

In part, this reductive notion of thinking receives an impetus from both cognitive psychology and neoclassical economics. The work of the first wave cognitivists, especially Piaget, conceptualized thinking in terms of developmental stages and mental *operations*. He was among the first to operationalize thinking and to define it according to stages of children's development.[3] Second wave cognitivists, picking up on the information-processing model of the mind, initiated by Claude Shannon's work in information theory, that began to model the mind on the brain by way of a strict analogy with the computer. This has led, in the third wave, to the study of thinking and the mind in terms of brain states, pursued in different ways by Howard Gardner (1983), who talks of 'multiple intelligences', and the Churchlands (1989; 1995), who talk of 'neural nets' (connectionism) and devise naturalised epistemologies.[4]

In neoclassicial economics, at least since the early 1960s, the notion of human capital theory has focused on human competences, which are taken to be both observable and measurable. First developed by Theodor Schultz (1971), an agri-cultural economist, and then taken up by Gary Becker (1992), the notion of human capital was theorised as key competences that were measurable for economic pur-poses. Becker himself indicates that when he first introduced the term in the 1960s there was near universal condemnation of it, and only 20 to 30 years later two US presidents, Reagan and Clinton, from opposing political parties, used the term as though it were a bipartisan affair. As the marketization of education proceeded during the 1980s the emphasis on human and social capital grew, as did the emphasis on the related concepts of entrepreneurship and enterprise.

First generation cognitive psychology and human capital theory shaped 'thinking' as a reductive concept, analysing it as stages, or as a set of intelligences, behav-iours, know-hows or skills. This approach, historically, might be usefully indexed and explained in part by reference to prevailing political economy—not only a strong emphasis on national competitiveness and on the 'core' generic skills of 'flexible workers' for the new globally networked economy, but also the flourishing of a range of new educational technologies and therapies focusing on 'accelerated learn-ing', 'giftedness', 'multiple intelligences' and the like.

Kinds of Thinking: Heidegger on *What is Called Thinking?*

In a strong sense philosophy has entertained a special relationship to thinking and reasoning: I suggested earlier that the history of reason is the history of philosophy itself. Kant defines philosophy as 'the science of the relation of all knowledge to the essential ends of human reason', or as 'the love which the reasonable being has for the supreme ends of human reason' (cited in Deleuze, 1984, p. 1). As Deleuze (1984, p. 1) himself reminds us, 'The supreme ends of Reason form the system of *Culture*; in these definitions we can already identify a struggle on two fronts: against empiricism and against dogmatic rationalism'.

Heidegger (1966, p. 3) begins his course of lectures, delivered during 1951 and 1952, with the following: 'We come to know what it means to think when we ourselves try to think. If the attempt is to be successful, we must be ready to learn thinking'.[5]

Learning, in other words, is central to understanding thinking. Yet, while there is an interest in philosophy, there is, he suggests, no 'readiness' to think. The fact is that, even though we live in the most thought-provoking age, 'we are still not thinking' (p. 4). In *What is Called Thinking?*, Heidegger is immediately concerned with learning and construes the learner on the model of the apprentice, emphasizing the notion of 'relatedness'—of the cabinet-maker's apprentice to the different kinds of wood that sustain the craft. The learner, by analogy, needs to learn different kinds of thinking.

In his Introduction to *Poetry, Language and Thought* (Heidegger, 1971) Albert Hofstadter refers to the language of Heidegger's thinking:

> It has created its own style, as always happens with an original thinker. Often a sentence or two is all that is necessary to distinguish Heidegger from, say, Wittgenstein, Russell or Whitehead. *The style is the thinking itself.* (p. xvi, emphasis added)

We should remember in passing that the later Heidegger in *Contributions to Philosophy* leads us to a post-philosophical project of 'thinking' where it is taken to mean precisely not that which defined the essence of the Western scientific tradition. Heidegger recognizes different kinds of thinking that have been defined by philosophers within the Western tradition. More importantly for our purposes here, in *What is Called Thinking?* He advances what we might take as a tentative typology of conceptions of thinking, before discussing his own conception. I have simply listed his suggestions and added Heidegger's own conceptions as well.

1. Thinking as *doxa*: forming an opinion or having an idea (opining).
2. Thinking as *'vorstellen'*: representing a state of affairs (representing).
3. Thinking as *ratiocination*: developing a chain of premises leading to a valid conclusion (reasoning).
4. Thinking as *problem-solving*: scientific thinking (problem-solving).
5. Thinking as *'beriff'* (Hegel): conceptual or systematic thinking (conceiving).
6. Thinking as *understanding or interpreting the particular* case in terms of the universal (practical judgement).
7. Thinking as a *revealing* of what is concealed (the meaning of Being) (Heidegger's thinking).
8. Thinking as *letting be* (the later Heidegger's post-metaphysical 'thinking').

We do not need to follow the entangled, mystical and poetic thought of the late Heidegger to understand that he usefully distinguishes different kinds of thinking that have defined the Western metaphysical tradition. All I need for my argument at this stage is the recognition of the historical fact of the diversity of notions of thinking: that there have in fact been dominant and prevailing notions of 'thinking' and that these have changed over time, although not in a progression of philosophical sophistication. We might, provocatively, add others to this list. I think we could usefully talk of various forms of cognitive modelling and computer simulation or information-processing as contemporary and technological views of thinking, although this might be considered a category mistake. Or we might, more productively, embrace the different views of Lyotard or Deleuze:

  9. Thinking as *information-processing* (cognitive psychology).
 10. Thinking as *suspicion of metanarratives*: narratology critique (Lyotard).
 11. Thinking as *creating concepts*: philosophizing (Deleuze).

This is not yet to naturalise thinking but simply to establish the case for different kinds of thinking—to pluralise it and to recognise its plurality: a range of different kinds, advanced by different philosophers at different points in the history of philosophy. From kinds of thinking to styles of reasoning, from Heidegger to Wittgenstein—this is the transition that we should now make.

Wittgenstein on Thinking

The work of the later Wittgenstein represents a break with the analytic tradition that is evidenced in Wittgenstein's rejection of both nominalism and the doctrine of external relations, and in Wittgenstein's view of philosophy as an activity—a pursuit separate from science, neither a second-order discipline nor foundational—which is unable to be characterized in terms of a distinctive method. Wittgenstein's liberation of grammar from logic, his rejection of any extra-linguistic justification for language and knowledge, and the 'semantic holism' of the *Investigations* (Wittgenstein, 1953) and *On Certainty* (Wittgenstein, 1979), simply collapses and renders impossible the set of distinctions (e.g. analytic/synthetic, scheme/content) upon which the legitimacy of analytic philosophy depends. For Wittgenstein there is no fundamental cleavage either between propositions that stand fast for us and those that do not, or between logical and empirical propositions. The whole enterprise of modern analytic philosophy rested on the fundamental 'Kantian' duality between scheme and content. Rorty (1980, p. 169) has moreover stressed the indispensability of the Kantian framework for modern analytic philosophy when he refers to the way distinctions between what is 'given' and what is 'added by the mind', or the distinction between the 'contingent' and the 'necessary' are required for a 'rational reconstruction' of our knowledge.

Rather than view Wittgenstein solely as a place-holder in the analytic tradition, it is philosophically and historically instructive to position him in terms of his Viennese origins and the general continental milieu that constituted his immediate intellectual and cultural background. Indeed, this rather obvious insight is, in large part, the basis for cultural, historical and literary readings of Wittgenstein and the significance of both the man and his work for education and pedagogy (see Peters & Marshall, 1999).

I have explored elsewhere the importance of style to philosophy through a study of Wittgenstein's *writings*: what I have called Wittgenstein's *styles of thinking*. I want to highlight the fact that the question of style remained an obsession of Wittgenstein's throughout his career—I have argued that it is inseparable from his practice of philosophy. In terms more fully explored elsewhere (Peters & Marshall, 1999), I have argued that Wittgenstein's 'style' is, in a crucial sense, *pedagogical*. By this I mean that appreciating his style is essential to understanding the purpose and intent of his philosophy, especially his later philosophy. In the context of the culture of Viennese modernism, I interpret Wittgenstein's philosophical style as related to his double crisis of identity concerning his Jewish origins and his sexuality, both inseparable from his concern for ethics and aesthetics and from his personal life. With Jim Marshall and Nick Burbules I have explored how these concerns are manifested in his work and his way of doing philosophy, and how Wittgenstein's style may be seen as deeply pedagogical (Peters & Marshall, 1999; see also Peters, Burbules & Smeyers, 2007).

More analytically, we can say that the early Wittgenstein of the *Tractatus* moves away from both mentalism, where thoughts are understood as psychic entities in the minds of individuals, and the Platonism of Frege and Russel, which was anti-psychologistic. The early Wittgenstein uses the concept *Gedanke*, or thought, in two related ways: as signifying a proposition (*Satz*), where it is taken to provide a 'logical picture of facts', and as a mental entity that stands in a relation to reality in much the same way as words stand to a propositional sign. Wittgenstein understood thinking to be a kind of language. Later he contended that the language of thought faced a dilemma, as Hans-Johann Glock notes:

> One the one hand, thought must be intrinsically representational. ... On the other hand, this means that the psychic elements do not stand in the same sort of relation to reality as words. More generally, Wittgenstein criticized the view that thinking is a mental process, which accompanies speech and endows it with meaning. (Glock, 1996, p. 358)

Glock suggests that Wittgenstein's mature position is to jettison both mentalism and his own lingualism of the *Investigations* to treat 'thinking' as 'a widely ramified concept' which has four major uses:

> (a) thinking about or meaning something; (b) reflecting on a problem; (c) believing or opining that *p*; (d) occurrent thoughts which cross one's mind at a particular moment. (Glock, 1996, p. 359)

Not only does Wittgenstein reject all forms of mentalism, but he links the notion of thinking to behaviour, suggesting that thinking is a mental *activity*: it is a *doing*, which is most often expressed in language. As a way of proceeding I suggest that we adopt Wittgenstein's notion of language games as a basis for understanding different kinds of thinking, based on making discursive 'moves' which we can represent in the following form:

1. Learning the rules of the game;
2. Learning to follow a rule by making 'moves' in the game (i.e. practical reason; *practice*);
3. Inventing a new 'move' in the game using existing rules;
4. Inventing a related series of moves (a new 'tactic' or 'strategy');
5. Inventing a new rule in the game;
6. Inventing a series of new rules, permitting new moves, tactics or strategies; and,
7. Inventing a new game.

Each of these 'stages' is subsumed by the next level, and clearly there is a hierarchy that operates. While this notion of thinking recognises *kinds of thinking*, it does so in a way that naturalises thinking to *playing* language games; in short, to the material conditions of discourse and to the mastery of its rules, tactics and strategies through use and practice.

One of the consequences of this typology is that it enables an historicization of reason to its material bases in discourses and discursive institutions in ways that have been adopted by discursive psychology and discourse theorists, following Wittgenstein and Foucault. This approach may permit us to investigate the history of reason and reasoning: for instance, the bifurcation of reason with Horkheimer into instrumental and practical reason; its typification as three under Habermas, with the development of critical reason; and finally, its multiplication in discourse use with Lyotard and Foucault. But these observations are only speculations aimed at an approach to the history of reason and styles of reasoning. It is a thought that I wish to pursue more systematically and in an exposition of some of the recent work of Ian Hacking.

Styles of Reasoning

In his Inaugural Lecture as the Chair of Philosophy and History of Scientific Concepts at the Collège de France in 2001, Hacking chose to develop the idea of *styles of reasoning*, which he credits to Ludwik Fleck. A Polish physician and epistemologist, Fleck developed highly original ideas on science in the 1920s and 1930s that were rediscovered in the 1960s and 1970s by Thomas Kuhn (1962) in his *The Structure of Scientific Revolutions*. Fleck basically suggested that 'scientific facts' are constructed by groups of scientists that he calls 'thought collectives'. These thought collectives are said to elaborate a 'thought style' containing norms, concepts and practices (cf. Kuhn's 'paradigms'). Thus, new members of the community become socialized into a specific *thought style* which shapes 'scientific facts' that may be 'incommensurable' with facts produced by other collectives. This incommensurability is seen by Fleck as an important source of innovation. Hacking argues that a style of reasoning introduces new ways of finding out the truth and also determines the truth conditions appropriate to the domains to which it applies. He writes:

> In the sciences we may use many styles of reasoning. Even within mathematics there is still something powerfully right about the distinction between arithmetic and geometry, or, we might better say, between algorithmic and combinatorial styles of reasoning, on the one hand, and on the other what we may loosely call the spatial style, be it geometrical, topological or making heavy use of symmetries. Undoubtedly the most powerful style of reasoning, that which has made possible the modern world, that which has permanently changed the world, large and small, that which is altering and engineering the world at this moment, is what I call the laboratory style, which was emerging four centuries ago. (Hacking, 2002a, pp. 2–3)

He offers the caution that 'there are many more styles of reasoning' (2002a, p. 3), emphasizing by way of example his own interest and work on the statistical style, and, by quoting Bourdieu, proceeds to defend a historical argument for the history of reason:

> We have to acknowledge that reason did not fall from heaven as a mysterious and forever inexplicable gift, and that it is therefore historical through and through; but we are not forced to conclude, as is often supposed, that it is reducible to history. It is in history, and in history alone, that we must seek the principle of the relative independence of reasons from the history of which it is a product; or, more precisely, in the strictly historical, but entirely specific logic through which the exceptional universes in which the singular history of reason is fulfilled were established. (cited in Hacking, 2002a, p. 3)

Hacking himself, picking up on Bourdieu's lead, argues that each style has its own proof and demonstration criteria, and it own truth conditions. For Hacking, then, a style of reasoning actually creates the truth criteria in a self-authenticating way. He argues (2002a, p. 4):

> Each scientific style of reasoning introduces a new domain of objects to study.
> Each style introduces a new class of objects, and on the side generates, for each new class of entities, a new realism/anti-realism debate. To stick to the most familiar examples, think of the reality of mathematical objects, with—in the extreme—the opposition between Platonism and mathematical constructivism.

He emphasizes classification as 'the essence of one style of scientific reasoning, and also something needed for thought itself', and considers some fundamental distinctions between classifications in the social and the natural sciences. He acknowledges that 'classification is at the core of the taxonomic sciences, of systematic botany and zoology' (2002a, p. 6), but asks which taxa are real. He discusses Duhem as someone 'committed to the idea of stable, growing and persistent natural classifications' (2002a, p. 7), putting him alongside Nietzsche in *The Gay Science*, whom he cites as follows:

> The fame, name and appearance of a thing, what it counts as, its customary measure and weight—which in the beginning is an arbitrary error for the most part, thrown over things like a garment and alien to their essence, even to their skin—due to the continuous growth of belief in it from generation to generation, gradually grows, as it were, onto and into the thing, and turns into its very body. (cited in Hacking, 2002a, p. 7)

Hacking continues his exposition of Nietzsche by reminding us that naming is an historical activity that takes place in particular sites at particular times. As he says, 'Objects come into being', and, signalling his own intellectual debt to Foucault—

whose ontology was both creative and historical—Hacking (2002a) mentions his book *Historical Ontology*, which is both a reflection on the uses of history in philosophy and an interpretation of the work of Foucault. In that work Hacking (2002b) entertains the concept of historical ontology by explaining how his work (and Foucault's) exemplify it. He also distinguishes it from 'historical epistemology' and 'historical meta-epistemology'. Drawing on the work of A. C. Crombie and what he calls 'styles of reasoning', Hacking advocates a conception of reason that is neither subjective nor constructivist. Many statements, he argues, including 'the maligned category of observation sentences', are independent of any given method of proof, and much of our scientific knowledge acquires determinate meaning in relation to specific styles of demonstration such as experimental, axiomatic, and analogical-comparative techniques. Styles of reasoning relativize what is knowable: they constitute a set of techniques both linguistic and material that make statements *candidates* for truth in the first place, and are therefore akin to Foucault's 'discourses'.

Hacking draws largely on Nelson Goodman's (1978) *Ways of Worldmaking* to articulate a theory of 'kind-making'. He credits Goodman with an original discovery with respect to the riddle of induction, which shows that:

> ... whenever we reach any general conclusion on the basis of evidence about its instances, we could, using the same rules of inference, but with different classifications, reach an opposite conclusion. (Hacking, 2002b, p. 128)

Goodman's conclusion, then, is the basis for Hacking's claim that we can and do inhabit many different worlds; he quotes Goodman to good effect:

> Without the organization, the selection of relevant kinds, effected by evolving tradition, there is no rightness or wrongness of categorization, no validity or invalidity of inductive inference, no fair or unfair sampling, and no uniformity or disparity among samples. (cited in Hacking, 2002b, p. 129)

He summarizes Goodman thus: 'The selection and organization of kinds determines ... what we call the world' and kinds come into being through a 'fit with practice ... effected by an evolving tradition' (2002b, p. 129). As for kinds, so analogically for classifications and names: as Hacking argues,

> Names work on us. They change us, they change how we experience our lives and how we choose our futures. ... They work in an immense world of practices, institutions, authorities, connotations, stories, analogies, memories, fantasies. ...
> An analysis of classifications of human beings is an analysis of classificatory words in the sites in which they are used, of the relations between speaker and hearer, of external descriptions and internal sensibilities. (2002a, p. 9)

Thus, the human and the social sciences do not differ from natural ones only because they socially construct their subjects, or because they require *Verstehen* rather than explanation. 'They differ because there is a dynamical interaction between the classifications developed in the social sciences, and the individuals or behavior classified' (2002a, p. 10).

If there is a payoff from Hacking's analysis that ought to be taken on board by educationalists, it is a kind of strong *interactive* classification that he refers to as *looping effects* in order to describe the fact that people who become aware of their classification have changed and can change themselves. He explains the notion of 'looping effects', which work by recursive feedback, by reference to the history of childhood. He suggests that in the wake of Philippe Ariès's famous *Centuries of Childhood* (1973), childhood has been called a social construct.

> Some people mean that the idea of childhood (and all that it implies) has been constructed. Others mean that a certain state of a person, or even a period in the life of a human being, an actual span of time, has been constructed. Some thinkers may even mean that children, as they exist today, are constructed. Children are conscious, self-conscious, very aware of their social environment, less articulate than many adults, perhaps, but, in a word, aware. People, including children, are agents, they act, as the philosophers say, under descriptions. The courses of action that they choose, and indeed their ways of being, are by no means independent of the available descriptions under which they may act. Likewise we experience ourselves in the world as being persons of various classifications. ... What was known about people classified in a certain way may become false because people so classified have changed in virtue of how they have been classified, what they believe about themselves, or because of how they have been treated as so classified. (Ariès, 1973, pp. 10–11)

Interactive classifications are a very common kind in education. Indeed, the literature abounds with interactive kinds—'accelerated learner', contrasted with 'slow learner' and 'recalcitrant learner'—all to do with the *speed* of learning, as though it characterizes a *kind* of learner. Yet this takes us further away from the second leg of the argument: styles of reasoning—not only *kinds* of thinking, but also *styles* of reasoning.

Such an interpretation and argument establishes the importance of philosophical accounts of thinking and reasoning and their assumed centrality to education, at least within the Western philosophical tradition. I have presented these accounts as both historical and pluralist. They introduce theoretical contestability into accounts of thinking that take us away from the pure realms of cognitive science and logic towards views that are historical, temporal, spatial, cultural, and, therefore, also empirical. We may recognise both *kinds of thinking* and *styles of reasoning*. If we do then a way opens to also recognising that new kinds of thinking and styles of reasoning come into existence and are developed and refined over time. This does not diminish their force or efficacy. It is analogously that the double blind experiment came into being at a particular time; that in a short duration it demonstrated a certain kind of efficacy in 'testing' that has not been surpassed; and, that the double blind experiment now represents a standard scientific practice: so too, with thinking and reasoning and their histories. The acceptance of this historical approach and plurality might serve as an antidote to the aggrandisement of one dominant form of thinking and reasoning in the field of education; it might also encourage a greater sensitivity to issues of discourse (or language games), their material conditions, and the rules that constitute them not only within and across the disciplines but also in their increasingly hybrid profusion.

Notes

1. In his *The Culture of Education* Bruner (1996) distinguishes the *culturalist theory of mind* from the computational theory, based on a model of information processing:

   > Culture, then, though itself man-made, both forms and makes possible the workings of a distinctively human mind. On this view, learning and thinking are always situated in a cultural setting and always dependent upon the utilization of cultural resources (Bruner, 1996, p. 4).

   He goes on to highlight the contrast between the culturalist and computational theory of mind in terms of a conception that embraces the tenets of *perspectivism* (the meaning of a statement is relative to its perspective), *constraints* (forms of meaning are constrained by our 'native endowment' and the nature of language), *constructivism* ('The "reality" we impute to "worlds" we inhabit is a constructed one' p. 19), *interaction* (intersubjectivity or the problem of knowing other minds), *externalisation* (the production of *oeuvres* or works), *instrumentalism* (the political context, e.g. education for skills), *institutionalism* (that education in the developed world takes place in institutions), *identity and self-esteem* (as he says, 'perhaps the most universal thing about human experience is the phenomenon of "Self", and we know that education is crucial for its formation' p. 35), and *narrative* (narrative as a mode of thought).
2. See the website http://www.criticalthinking.org/. On review and critique, see Biesta and Stams, 2001; Weinstein at http://www.chss.montclair.edu/inquiry/fall95/weinste.html; Burbules and Park at http://faculty.ed.uiuc.edu/burbules/papers/critical.html and Hatcher at http://www.bakeru.edu/crit/literature/dlh_ct_critique.htm
3. There is now a growing literature on 'post-formal thinking', which Ken Wilbur (1995) configures as *postmodern* (which is radically contextual) and postulates in terms of the evolution of holistic thinking (which is integrative). Formal operations are said to overemphasize the power of pure logic in problem solving and underemphasize the pragmatic quality of real life cognitive activity. By contrast, post-formal thought emphasizes 'shifting gears', multiple causality, multiple solutions, pragmatism and awareness of paradox. See Labouvie-Vief, 1980; Sinnott, 1998 and Marchland, 2001.
4. Neural networks are simplified models of the brain that measure the strength of connections between neurons. Against the classical view that human cognition is analogous to symbolic computation in digital computers, the connectionist claims that information is stored non-symbolically in the strength of connections between the units of a neural net. Gardner defines intelligence as 'the capacity to solve problems or to fashion products that are valued in one or more cultural setting' (Gardner & Hatch, 1989). Using biological as well as cultural research, he formulated a list of seven intelligences: logical-mathematical, linguistic, spatial, musical, bodily-kinesthetic, intra- and inter-personal, and naturalist. The notion of 'styles of thinking' also has been used as a predictor of academic performance and discussed in terms of multiple intelligences. Various integrative models have been proposed: Curry's (1983) personality model; Miller's (1987) model of cognitive processes; Riding and Cheema's (1991) model of cognitive styles; and Sternberg's (1997) model as a theory of mental self-government, which delineates thirteen styles.
5. This section, which refers to *What is Called Thinking?*, draws on Peters, 2002a.

References

Ariès, P. (1973) *Centuries of Childhood* (New York, Jonathan Cape).

Becker, G. (1992) *Human Capital: A theoretical and empirical analysis with special reference to education* (Chicago; London, University of Chicago Press).

Biesta, G. & Stams, G. (2001) Critical Thinking and the Question of Critique: Some lessons from deconstruction, *Studies in Philosophy and Education*, 20:1, pp. 74–92.

Bruner, J. (1996) *The Culture of Education* (Cambridge, MA, Harvard University Press).

Churchland, P. S. (1989) *A Neurocomputational Perspective: The nature of mind and the structure of science* (Cambridge, MA, MIT Press).

Churchland, P. M. (1995) *The Engine of Reason, the Seat of the Soul: A philosophical journey into the brain* (Cambridge, MA, MIT Press).

Curry, L. (1983) An Organization of Learning Styles Theory and Constructs, ERIC Document 235, p. 185.

Deleuze, G. (1984) *Kant's Critical Philosophy: The doctrine of the faculties*, trans. H. Tomlinson & B. Habberjam (Minneapolis, University of Minnesota Press).

Gardner, H. (1983) *Frames of Mind: The theory of multiple intelligences* (New York, Basic Books).

Gardner, H. & Hatch, T. (1989) Multiple Intelligences Go to School: Educational implications of the theory of multiple intelligences, *Educational Researcher*, 18:8, pp. 4–10.

Gergen, K. (1985) The Social Constructionist Movement in Modern Psychology, *American Psychologist*, 40, pp. 266–75.

Gergen, K. (1991) *The Saturated Self: Dilemmas of identity in contemporary life* (New York, Basic Books).

Gergen, K. (2001) *Social Construction in Context* (Thousand Oaks, CA; London, Sage Publications).

Glock, H-J. (1996) *A Wittgenstein Dictionary* (Oxford, Blackwell).

Goodman, N. (1978) *Ways of Worldmaking* (Indianapolis, Hackett).

Habermas, J. (1987) *Knowledge & Human Interest*, (orig. 1968), trans. J. Shapiro (London, Polity Press).

Hacking, I. (2000) *The Social Construction of What?* (Cambridge, MA, Harvard University Press).

Hacking, I. (2002a) Inaugural Lecture: Chair of philosophy and history of scientific concepts at the Collège de France, 16 January 2001, *Economy and Society*, 31:1, pp. 1–14.

Hacking, I. (2002b) *Historical Ontology* (Cambridge, MA, Harvard University Press).

Harré, R. & Gillet, G. (1994) *The Discursive Mind* (Thousand Oaks, CA; London, Sage Publications).

Heidegger, M. (1966) *Discourse on Thinking*. A Translation of Gelassenheit by J. M. Anderson and E. H. Freund, with an Introduction by J. M. Anderson (New York, Harper Torchbooks).

Heidegger, M. (1971) *Poetry, Language and Thought*, trans. and ed. A Hofstadter (New York, Harper & Row).

Heidegger, M. (1977) *The Question Concerning Technology and Other Essays*, trans. W. Lovitt. (New York, Harper & Row, 1977).

Howie, D. & Peters, M. A. (1996) Positioning Theory: Vygotsky, Wittgenstein and social constructionist psychology, *Journal for the Theory of Social Behaviour*, 26:1, pp. 51–64.

Kuhn, T. (1962) *The Structure of Scientific Revolutions* (Chicago, University of Chicago Press).

Labouvie-Vief, G. (1980) Beyond Formal Operations: Uses and limits of pure logic in lifespan development, *Human Development*, 23, pp. 114–146.

Marchland, H. (2001) Some Reflections On PostFormal Thought, *The Genetic Epistemologist*, 29:3.

Miller, A. (1987) Cognitive Styles: An integrated model, *Educational Psychology*, 7, pp. 251–268.

Peters, M. A. (2000) *Pós-estruturalismo e filosofia da diferença Uma introdução* (Belo Horizonte, Autêntica Editora). (*Poststructuralism and the Philosophy of Difference: An introduction*), trans. into Portuguese by T. Tadeu Da Silva.

Peters, M. A. (2000) Writing the Self: Wittgenstein, confession and pedagogy, *Journal of Philosophy of Education*, 34:2, pp. 353–368.

Peters, M. A. (2001a) Philosophy as Pedagogy: Wittgenstein's styles of thinking. *Radical Pedagogy*, 3:3 (http://www.icaap.org/iuicode?2.3.3.4).

Peters, M. A. (2001b) Wittgensteinian Pedagogics: Cavell on the figure of the child in the *Investigations*, *Studies in Philosophy and Education*, 20, pp. 125–138.

Peters, M. A. (2002a) (ed.) *Heidegger, Education and Modernity* (Lanham, Boulder, NY, Oxford, Rowman & Littlefield).

Peters, M. A. (2002b) Nietzsche's Legacy for Education Revisited, *Studies in Philosophy and Education*, forthcoming.

Peters, M. A. (2002c) Wittgenstein, Education and the Philosophy of Mathematics, *Theory and Science*, 3:3 (http://theoryandscience.icaap.org/).

Peters, M. A. (2003a) The University and the New Humanities: Professing with Derrida', *Arts and Humanities in Higher Education*, 3:1, pp. 41–57.

Peters, M. A. (2003b) Truth-telling as an Educational Practice of the Self: Foucault, *parrhesia* and the ethics of subjectivity, *Oxford Review of Education*, 29:2, pp. 207–223.

Peters, M. A. (2003c) Geophilosophy, Education and the Pedagogy of the Concept, *Educational Philosophy and Theory*, 36:3, pp. 217–226.

Peters, M. A. & Appel, S. (1996) Positioning Theory: Discourse, the subject and the problem of desire', *Social Analysis*, 40:September, pp. 120–145.

Peters, M. A., Burbules, N. & Smeyers, P. (2007) *Saying and Showing: Wittgenstein as pedagogical philosopher* (Lanham, MD & Oxford, Paradigm Publishers).

Peters, M. A., Lankshear, C. & Olssen, M. (eds) (2003a) *Critical Theory: Founders and praxis* (New York, Peter Lang).

Peters, M. A., Lankshear, C. & Olssen, M. (eds) (2003b) *Futures of Critical Theory: Dreams of difference* (Lanham, Boulder, NY, Oxford, Rowman & Littlefield).

Peters, M. A. & Marshall, J. D. (1999) *Wittgenstein: Philosophy, postmodernism, pedagogy* (Westport, CT & London, Bergin & Garvey).

Peters, M. A., Marshall, J. D. & Smeyers, P. (2001) (eds) *Nietzsche's Legacy for Education: Past and present values* (Westport, CT. & London, Bergin & Garvey).

Riding, R. J. & Cheema, I. (1991) Cognitive styles—An overview and integration, *Educational Psychology*, 11:3 & 4, pp. 193–215.

Schultz, T. (1971) *Investment in Human Capital: The role of education and of research* (New York, Free Press).

Shotter, J. (1993) Harré, Vygotsky, Bakhtin, Vico, Wittgenstein; Academic discourses and conversational realities, *Journal for the Theory of Social Behaviour*, 23, pp. 459–82.

Sinnott, J. D. (1998) *The Development of Logic in Adulthood: Postformal thought and its applications* (New York, Plenum).

Sternberg, R. J. (1997) *Thinking Styles* (New York, Cambridge University Press).

Wilbur, K. (1995) *Sex, Ecology, Spirituality* (Boston, Shambhala).

Wittgenstein, L. (1953) *Philosophical Investigations*, trans. G. E. M. Anscombe (Oxford, Blackwell).

Wittgenstein, L. (1979) *On Certainty*, edited by G. E. M. Anscombe & G. H. Von Wright (Oxford, Blackwell).

3

Culture, Cognitive Pluralism and Rationality

COLIN W. EVERS
Faculty of Education, The University of Hong Kong

Introduction

The aim of this paper is to explore the prospects for objectivity in reasoning strategies in light of a number of empirical studies on how people actually reason, particularly where these studies show that there are systematic culture-based differences in patterns of reasoning. In broad outline, the argument I shall propose is as follows.

First, some well-known results from empirical psychology will be presented that show that there are important differences between, on the one hand, how people actually reason on certain simple cognitive tasks, and on the other hand, what the best reasoning is in these tasks. In response to these findings, which suggest that people are irrational in certain respects, or subject to cognitive illusions, two types of argument against the possibility of systematic human irrationality will be considered.

Second, it will be shown that these arguments are vulnerable to evidence of culture-based differences in cognition. Salient features of this evidence will then be reviewed, together with a key argument that attempts to show that evidence for cognitive pluralism implies normative cognitive pluralism, that is, that there are multiple, divergent standards of good reasoning.

Finally, I shall argue that there is at least one modest class of exceptions to the claim that there are alternative, equally warranted standards of good reasoning. This concerns the task of solving certain well-structured problems. Suitably chosen, these, I suggest, are common, or touchstone, to the sorts of culturally different viewpoints discussed. As a consequence, a normative view of reasoning and, by implication, critical thinking can be defended, at least relative to this cross-cultural touchstone.

Reviewing the Arguments

Evidence for Human Irrationality

There is a substantial body of literature in empirical psychology that reports analyses and findings about how people reason. Typically, such studies employ well-defined cognitive tasks about which good and bad reasoning can easily be adjudicated. Perhaps the most frequently discussed is what is known as the *selection task*, first devised by Peter Wason (1966) and designed to test an understanding of logical relations. The task consists of four cards with a letter on one side and a number on the other. Two are shown with the letter face up, two with the number face up, thus:

A   B   7   6

Experiment participants are then invited to say which cards have to be turned over in order to determine the truth of the claim: 'If a card has a vowel on one side, then it has an odd number on the other side' (Samuels & Stich, 2004, p. 280). Participants—usually university undergraduates—have no trouble choosing the 'A' card. But then many fail to choose the '6' card since they do not realize that its failure to have a consonant on the other side would falsify the truth of the conditional. That is, people fail to see that 'if x then y' is equivalent, by *modus tollens*, to 'if ~y then ~x'.

One explanation for this failure that has been explored by a number of writers—e.g. D'Andrade (1989) and Hutchins (2005)—is that people can make correct logical inferences if the problems they are dealing with are embedded in culturally coherent mental schemas. Thus, if participants are shown the premise 'If x is true then y is true', and they are told 'y is not true' and invited to choose, among alternatives, what follows logically from that, only 15% of respondents in the study chose correctly 'x is not true' as their answer. On the other hand if participants are given the premise 'If this is a garnet, then it is a semi-precious stone', and told 'This is not a semi-precious stone', they have no trouble choosing, from among alternatives, the correct answer 'This is not a garnet' (Hutchins, 2005, p. 1558).

The suggested difference between cognitively processing the abstract premise, with its x's and y's, and the premise about the semi-precious stone is that 'unless x and y are associated with particular known concepts, our culture has nothing in particular to say about the relationship between x and y' (Hutchins, 2005, p. 1558). A coherent linking of concepts for x and y, however, allows the transformations involving x into y, y into ~y and ~y into ~x to be held stably in memory while the inferences are performed.

Another well-studied cognitive illusion concerns how people reason about probability. Tversky and Kahneman (1982) presented participants in an experiment with the following description of Linda:

> Linda is 31 years old, single, outspoken, and very bright. She majored in philosophy. As a student, she was deeply concerned with issues of discrimination and social justice, and also participated in anti-nuclear demonstrations. (Tversky & Kahneman, 1982, p. 92)

Participants were then asked to rank from most probable to least probable a set of eight statements about Linda. The key result was that most people thought that 'Linda is a bank teller and is active in the feminist movement' to be more probably true than the statement 'Linda is a bank teller', even though a conjunction of two features is never more probable than either of the features.

Here, the explanation for this result, which was robust, holding up over many trials, was that people thought of Linda in terms of prototypes, where a prototype is a cluster of features that coheres in a characteristic way. It is the plausibility of the prototype that misleads over the probability of the conjunction of features.

Notice that just as the absence of culturally coherent mental models functioned as an explanation for poor cognitive performance on abstract logical reasoning tasks, so the presence of culturally coherent mental models, in the form of proto-types, is claimed to be responsible for errors over probability judgments. Evidently, to improve human reasoning on these and many other tasks, it is vital to possess normatively appropriate representations, or mental models, something that the empirical literature implies many of us do not possess.

Some Philosophical Responses

In response to this pessimistic prognosis, there are several important philosophical arguments that attempt to show that the very concept of systematic human irrationality is incoherent. These arguments do not deny that some errors of reasoning occur. Rather they deny the possibility of error being endemic in human thought.

The first group of arguments focuses around the methodology of attributing conceptual schemes to people. In one that was much discussed in the 1960s, Quine (1960, pp. 26–79) explores the conditions that determine how to do radical language translation, in particular, how to translate an unknown language into English with no more resources except observational evidence about the conditions under which utterances are made and responded to. One of the maxims he empha-sizes for translating logical connectives is that any translation that posits the speaker to hold wildly implausible views is more likely to be a mistranslation than a confusion in the mind of the speaker: 'The common sense behind the maxim is that one's interlocutor's silliness, beyond a certain point, is less likely than bad translation ...' (1960, p. 59). Without the assumption of some minimal rationality, there are insufficient constraints on translation to make the job meaningful. Almost anything will count as an adequate translation if we cannot impose the condition that a translation preserves for the speaker a coherent scheme of thought.

Donald Davidson (1984) offers similar considerations in understanding what others are saying. Suppose you use the word 'proton' everywhere that I would use the word 'electron'. For you, protons are negatively charged particles that occupy places in a configuration around an atom's nuclear material. For me it is electrons that do that. The same for atomic weights, quantum spin number, and so on. At some point, it is more reasonable to assume that you have a coherent world view, similar to mine, and that the difference between us is purely linguistic: you are ascribing truth to the same claims that I do and are merely using the word 'proton' where I would use the word 'electron'. Indeed, Davidson goes further. In order to interpret the utterances of another about, say, atomic theory, we are obliged to assume some broad agreement of truths between us. He thinks that charity in interpreting others 'is forced on us; whether we like it or not, if we want to understand others, we must count them right in most matters' (Davidson, 1984, p. 197). This implies that conceptual relativism is false; we cannot make sense of the idea that different cultures have radically different conceptual schemes. Instead, the business of interpretation proceeds by reading our requirements for the truth of their claims into the process of translation. Thus, their beliefs are as coherent as ours if we interpret their 'proton' as our 'electron'.

Daniel Dennett (1978) imposes sterner requirements on the link between inter-pretation of a person's beliefs and desires, of their intentionality, and rationality. In order to make sense of the behavior of people, he supposes we posit them as possessing a coordinated framework of beliefs and desires. So when you go to the fridge to retrieve a beer, I understand that behavior in terms of positing your desire for a beer and your belief that the beer is in the fridge. That is, the fridge-going behavior, construed as intentional behavior, is a rational consequence of the link between the belief and the desire. But according to Dennett (1978, p. 20), 'when a person falls short of perfect rationality ... there is no coherent intentional descrip-tion' of a person's mental states.

The core claims being made by these arguments are that we cannot do radical translation, or we cannot impute conceptual schemes, or we cannot impute inten-tional behavior without also imputing a large amount of rationality to people's words, thoughts and behavior.

There are several points that I would like to make in response. First, with the possible exception of Dennett's requirements, the amount of imputed rationality seems to be fairly fault tolerant. Problems with *modus tollens* or probability assign-ments seem to be easily detectable in the process of interpretation, perhaps owing to the fact that under the given experimental conditions, normative standards of rationality are not in question. Participants' judgments are clearly errors. Of course, once cognitive tasks move beyond examples from toy universes into those that offer more complex challenges, such as multi-criterial decision-making, the adjudication of rationality becomes more controversial.

Second, despite their talk of rationality and coherence, these arguments fail to achieve a defense of a unitary conception of rationality. Rather, they merely imply that the interpreter must project his or her concept of rationality into the task of making sense of others. But as Stephen Stich (1990) often asks: Whose concept of rationality is being used? For there are very many possible concepts of rationality that can be invoked, from individuals with their idiosyncratic differences to whole societies with broad cultural differences. The shift to a more ubiquitous concept may again be due to background agreement about the data exhibiting evidence of reasoning errors.

An influential argument that purports to settle this matter, and establish a unitary view of human reason, has been offered by Jonathan Cohen (1981). To deal with the objection that lapses in human reasoning compromise the claim that humans are fundamentally rational, Cohen distinguishes between competence and perform-ance in much the same way that linguists draw the distinction. Mistakes in reason-ing are like uttering the occasional ungrammatical sentence—they are performance errors made under particular circumstances that occur against a broader context of underlying, or tacit, reasoning competence. That is, people possess the capacity to reason well but circumstances such as distractions or forgetting prevent that capacity from being manifested. Rules of inference are part of our reasoning capacity as rules of grammar are part of our linguistic capacity.

But why should this tacit knowledge of rules of inference be normatively appropriate, given the evidence for human irrationality? Cohen's answer is that these tacit rules arise out of a process of reflective equilibrium. We revise our intuitions about rules if they lead to inferential consequences we cannot accept, and we revise our views about the unacceptability of consequences if they are entailed by rules that we cannot revise. (See also Stich, 1990, pp. 79–86.) Now if reflective equilibrium yields all of the justification there is to be had, if there is no justification procedure for reasoning beyond that emerging from the processes of reflective equilibrium, then the empirical evidence for posits of rational competence is the same as that given in descriptions of human reasoning performance in all their variegated detail.

Needless to say, this argument has been extensively discussed and debated. (See, for example, Open Peer Commentary, 1981, pp. 331–359.) For our purposes, we can again ask the question: Whose rationality is in reflective equilibrium? Because the acquisition of rationality, in common with most learning, is mediated by wider social processes beyond the level of the individual, where a person reaches what appears to be an idiosyncratic equilibrium, it may be easier to argue the case that this is a matter of performance errors than a lack of competence. However, where entire cultural traditions settle into equilibria that manifest as judgments contrary to the sorts of simple normative reasoning rules captured by *modus tollens* or elementary probability theory, the distinction between performance errors and reasoning competence becomes more problematic.

Cultural Differences in Reasoning

There is an extensive body of empirical research on cultural differences in reasoning that has been gathered and analyzed by Richard Nisbett and his co-authors. In a major review of findings on patterns of reasoning among East Asians and Westerners (mainly North Americans), they offer the following summary:

> The authors find East Asians to be holistic, attending to the entire field and assigning causality to it, making relatively little use of categories and formal logic, and relying on 'dialectical' reasoning, whereas Westerners are more analytic, paying attention primarily to the object and the categories to which it belongs and using rules, including formal logic, to understand behaviour. (Nisbett *et al.*, 2001, p. 291)

Although their review contains many kinds of examples to illustrate their thesis, two in particular can be singled out for discussion. The first, what they regard as 'one of the best established findings in cognitive social psychology' is the 'fundamental attribution error, ... the tendency to see behaviour as a product of the actor's dispositions and to ignore important situational determinants of the behaviour' (Nisbett *et al.*, 2001, p. 298).

Here's an example of an experiment that purports to show evidence of cultural differences in causal attribution. The first part of the experiment sets the scene. Consider a situation in which participants, both Americans and Koreans, are invited to read an essay that either supports or opposes some important social issue. Participants are told that the author of the essay had no choice in determining what view to take. They then have to say what the author really believed about the issue. Those reading the affirmative essay were much more inclined to say that the author believed the affirmative position than those who had read the opposing essay. In the second stage of the experiment, participants themselves were asked to write such an essay and given no choice as to which side of the issue they took. They were then told that the author of the essay they were to read had been though a similar 'no choice' situation. Once again, participants were asked to indicate what view the author held. For the American participants, the experience of having to write such an essay themselves made no difference in their willingness to attribute affirmative views to the author. But for the Korean participants, their identical experience made a substantial difference. The Americans appeared to be assuming a narrower, more individualistic, causal field for their attribution judgments, while the Koreans took a more holistic perspective in which factors outside the individual were relevant (Choi & Nisbett, 1998; Nisbett *et al.*, 2001, pp. 298–299).

Although the evidence for a performance error of causal attribution may be utterly ambiguous in a scaled up complex world, in the restricted universe of this experimental set-up, it is normatively clear.

A different set of examples, one removed from attributions, concerns the assessment of arguments and argument strategies. Here is one study that again uses Korean and American participants, this time university students. Two sorts of logic exercises were constructed for the groups. The first consisted of a set of abstract syllogisms with no content. The second consisted of a set of meaningful syllogisms with both plausible and implausible conclusions. The task was to classify the syllogisms as either valid or invalid. Both groups performed equally well on the abstract syllogisms, but on the second task, Korean students showed a stronger belief bias than American students. That is, they were more willing to classify valid arguments as invalid if the arguments had an implausible conclusion. '[T]he results indicate that when logical structure conflicts with everyday belief, American students are more willing to set aside empirical belief in favour of logic than are Korean students' (Nisbett *et al.*, 2001, p. 301).

In another study, American participants who were persuaded to accept the conclusion of a strong argument, became even more convinced of the conclusion if a weak argument was presented that contradicted the conclusion. East Asian participants, on the other hand, became less convinced of the conclusion in those circumstances (Nisbett *et al.*, 2001, p. 302).

If these sorts of studies provide any indication of culture-wide reasoning processes, then it is plausible to suppose that what can arise out of reflective equilibrium can be at odds with normative rationality.

Normative Cognitive Pluralism

In a wide-ranging discussion of all these issues, Stich (1990) draws a more radical conclusion. He thinks that empirical evidence for cultural diversity in cognitive practices undermines claims to there being just one normative standard of rationality. His argument is complex since he considers a variety of philosophical positions, but the core idea is this. Consider how one would defend a candidate set of norms of rationality. Presumably some justificatory arguments would need to be made that involved appeal to reasons. Let's call these reasons 'second order reasons'. But now a regress threatens, because second order reasons have to come from somewhere. And unless they can be quarantined, or shown to enjoy some special privileged cognitive status, they will be affected by the same processes of reflective equilibrium that apply to the first order culture-laden reasons. But the empirical data on human reasoning shows that reflective equilibrium does not logically guarantee normative appropriateness. Hence, the second order principles of rationality required to justify first order principles of rationality are not known to be normatively appropriate (Stich, 1990, pp. 89–100).

Stich explores various strategies for dealing with the problem. For example, he considers the idea that there may be some conceptual link between the nature of rationality, which would have normative force, and some proposed collection of second order reasoning principles. Unfortunately, concepts have to come from somewhere too, and are subject just as much to culture-ladenness as are reasons. Views of rationality, defended in this way, are in the same boat as principles used to justify principles.

Another possible defense of second order principles of reasoning is a consequentialist approach: for example, choose those principles that lead to the most satisfactory outcomes. It seems unlikely, however, that the specification of satisfactory outcomes can proceed in a cultural vacuum. And yet, the principles of elementary logic and probability theory that provided such a useful normative corrective to commonly made inferences about Linda the bank teller or the selection task are unlikely to lose their utility where people want to navigate their way through life making decisions whose outcomes are more reliably known than those based on the toss of a coin.

Building on the apparent capacity of these modest tools for being pressed into wider service of utility, the strategy that I wish to pursue here develops the thought that there may be enough structure in some of the problems that different groups face to defend a view of reason that can have normative force across these groups.

Problems, Solutions and Objectivity

Well Structured Problems

In his dialogue, the *Meno*, Plato asks the question 'How is inquiry possible?' and poses a paradox in response. If we know what it is we seek then we have no need for inquiry. But if we don't know what it is we seek, then we would never know if

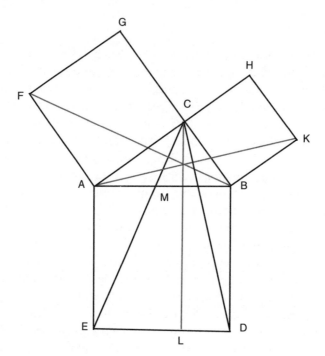

Figure 1: Euclid's first proof that $AB^2 = AC^2 + BC^2$

we found it. Therefore inquiry is either unnecessary or pointless. For Plato, the way out of the dilemma was to say that inquiry was really just recollection of what we already knew. And to prove his point, the dialogue shows how a slave boy, under close questioning, knows the proof of Pythagoras' Theorem. Herbert Simon (1977), in the company of many others, has proposed another resolution, one that involves arguing that we know we have found what we seek when it solves the problem we are inquiring to solve. (See also Haig, 1987, for a discussion of this matter.) The more well structured the problem, the easier it is to know that we have a solution. Finding the length of the hypotenuse of a right-angled triangle, given the lengths of the other two sides, is a case in point. The most famous proof is probably Euclid's first proof. It proceeds by constructing squares on each side of the triangle. Lines are then added to the resulting figure to create additional triangles. By a series of reasoning steps, it is shown that the sum of the areas of the smaller squares is equal to the area of the larger square (Figure 1).

The reasoning is as follows. The area of triangle ABK is half the square BCHK and also equals the area of triangle CBD which equals half LD × DB. Similarly, the area of triangle AFB is half the square AFGC and also equals the area of triangle AEC which equals half AE × EL. But EL + LD equals AE, the side of the largest square. So BCHK plus AFGC equals AEDB.

Perhaps the earliest proof on record is that given by ancient Chinese mathematicians, by some estimates as early as 1100BC, although a more generally accepted date is the 6th century BC. Known as the '*Gougu* Theorem' in traditional Chinese geometry, and appearing in both the *Zhou Bi* and *Jui Zhang* texts, the strategy (illustrated in Figure 2)

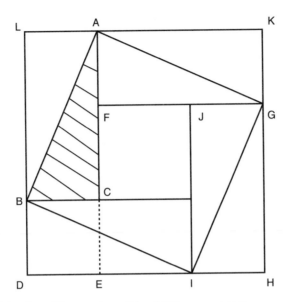

Figure 2: Strategy of the *Gougu* Theorem in traditional Chinese geometry

is slightly different, although again it involves showing that the areas of squares drawn on the sides of the triangle add in the required way (Wu, 1983, pp. 70–72).

Here's the reasoning. BDEC is the square on the 'gou', or shorter, arm, while EFGH is equal to the square on the 'gu' or longer arm. Now from the figure BDHGFC, which is the sum of the squares of these two arms, cut the triangle BDI and place it at AFG, to make the new square ABIG, which is the square of the hypotenuse.

The problem of finding the length of the hypotenuse of a right angle triangle given the lengths of the other two sides is sufficiently well structured to admit of the same answer, although often via different proofs, regardless of culture or history.

There is also a surprising amount of structure in physics problems, as can be seen even when two fundamentally different worldviews are in dispute. For example, against an Aristotelian view of motion, which was the dominant position in his cultural landscape, Galileo employed a very minimalist argument that made use of premises embedded in the structure of both that view and his opposing perspective. A consequence of Aristotelian dynamics was a theory of inertia that implied that heavy objects fall faster than light ones. Against this, Galileo devised the following thought experiment. (See Popper, 1957, pp. 442–443.)

Begin by hypothesizing that heavier objects fall faster than light objects. Imagine two masses, M and m, connected by a light inelastic string (Figure 3).

Let us suppose that the heavy object, M, begins to fall rapidly, with velocity V_M, on being released, but its downward motion is then impeded by the slower motion, V_m, of the lesser mass, m, to which it is tethered. The two masses connected by the string thus move more slowly than the heavier mass alone and faster than the lesser mass. Let us wind in the string. When separated by an infinitely small distance, the total moves more slowly than the larger mass, but when the two objects meet, by hypothesis, their velocity, V_{M+m}, should exceed that of the larger mass. Since the string can be made

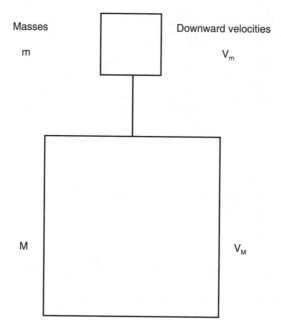

Masses   Downward velocities

m V_m

M V_M

Figure 3: Galileo's thought experiment

vanishingly small, this implies that, in the limit, the combined mass is moving both faster and more slowly, which is a contradiction. Therefore the Aristotelian hypothesis is false.

That such a powerful empirical conclusion can emerge from such modest premises, including principles of reasoning that were common to both worldviews, is a lesson in how important structure can be. Popper (1957, p. 443), in his commentary on this reasoning, says: 'I see in Galileo's imaginary experiment a perfect model for the best use of imaginary experiments'.

In addition to mathematics and physics, a vast amount of technology is heavily constrained by the way the world is, rather than simply by culture or individual mindset. (For an impressive inventory of ancient Chinese inventions, Joseph Needham's multivolume work, *Science and Civilization in China*, should be consulted.) The technology for providing a water supply for ancient cities needed to come to terms with water's key properties, including its propensity to flow downhill. This constrained the design of aqueducts in the Roman world, and prompted the invention of water-locks for canals in China. Developments in transportation, agriculture, metallurgy, currency, bridge and building construction, shipbuilding, navigation, moveable print presses, the spinning wheel and the loom are all similarly constrained by the properties of the materials that figure in their construction and composition. The fact that many of these ideas and inventions arose independently in different times, places and cultures, again points to the existence of common constraints that define problems and similarities among ways of reaching solutions, including cognitive ways and means. Whatever the theoretical limits of cognitive pluralism, its practical limits are clearly evident, unless there are grounds for thinking the similarities are entirely accidental.

To explore this matter a little further, we need to take a closer look at how problems and solutions might be characterized. I begin with Thomas Nickles, who asks the question 'What, then, are problems?' and responds:

> My short answer is that a problem consists of *all* the conditions or *constraints* on the solution plus the demand that the solution (an object satisfying the constraints) be found. For this reason ... , I call it the *constraint-inclusion model* of problems. The constraints characterize—in a sense 'describe'—the sought-for solution. (Nickles, 1981, p. 109)

The first point to note about this answer is that it does not rule out different ways of solving a problem within a given constraint set. Thus, there are currently some forty different ways of proving Pythagoras' Theorem. They all yield the same result, but some manage to be strikingly different while still falling within touchstone, or common, or agreed requirements for mathematical proof.

However, there is another source of difference that is more substantial. It concerns the prioritizing, or ranking, of constraints. Take a simple decision problem: whether to make a big move of household in order to take a better job. There are various constraints: the attraction of more money, more prestige, and more interesting challenges. Then there are the difficulties of making the move, disrupting one's family, giving up valuable friendships, and so on (Thagard & Millgram, 1995, p. 446). The solution that different people come to—whether to take the job or not—will depend on the different priorities or levels of importance they attach to the various considerations. That is, this conception of ranking determines, to some extent, the structure of a web of belief, with least revisable or most heavily prioritized claims towards the centre of the web and more revisable ones at the periphery. Cultural differences can present in the form of systematic differences in priorities to the point where solutions can be characteristically different. Research on Chinese and American approaches to management problems, for example, implies that maintaining harmony in the workplace acts as a more powerful priority, and hence constraint, on the decisions that Chinese managers make than it does on their American counterparts (Wong, 2001).

The way to deal with this issue would be to see the rationality of solving problems by satisfying constraints as a process that operates in much the same way regardless of the priorities people assign to claims or the different weights they give to the constraints. Then the cognitive task boils down to trying to secure a kind of 'best fit', or most coherent course of action. Of course, not everyone would actually behave in this way. But not everyone assigns the normatively appropriate probabilities to the descriptions of Linda the bank teller either. So the normative requirement here is to solve problems that your own system of priorities says are worth solving, in a way that respects the priorities that define the problem.

Problems of Scale

Whether this can be done with large-scale problems is a difficult issue. As a refinement of Nickles's analysis that involves some further reconceptualization of key terms, consider a proposal by Thagard and Verbeurgt (1998) for computing best fit in a constraint satisfaction theory choice model. Imagine that we have a set of claims, E, that contains the following elements: e_1, e_2, e_3, ... e_n. Suppose that some of these claims, say e_i and e_j, are positively constrained in the sense that we can accept both or reject both, or negatively constrained, in the sense that if we accept one we would want to reject the other. So, if e_i explains e_j then we would want to accept (or reject) both, whereas if e_i is contradicted by e_j, we would want to accept one and reject the other. Let the strength of the link between two positively or negatively constrained elements, e_i and e_j, be called the weight, w_{ij}, of the pair. Now a best fit on the set of claims E, is a partition of its elements that maximizes some way of summing of all the weights.

One way in which Thagard (1992) implements this abstract model in computer simulations of real theory choice problems in the history of science is by treating it as a harmony artificial neural network, as follows. Each proposition of a theory, or its main rival, e_i, corresponds to a node in the network. The initial priority, or importance, of the proposition would be given by its level of activation, a_i, at that node. The weights, w_{ij}, between nodes correspond to the influence one node has on the activation of another node. A best fit choice of theory would be those nodes with higher activation values that emerged subject to the requirement to maximize the sum of all the weighted products of pairs of activation values:

$$\text{Best Fit} = \text{Maximizing } \Sigma_i \Sigma_j w_{ij} a_i a_j.$$

The idea is that over the duration of learning a best fit solution, some nodes will be turned off and some will be increased, leaving the active nodes representing a maximally coherent set of true propositions.

From a computational perspective, the main problem is the sheer number of calculations that have to be performed. For n propositions, the computer would have to calculate 2^n possible solutions (Thagard & Verbeurgt, 1998, pp. 7–8). In general, mathematical modeling of constraint satisfaction problems for even a relatively modest set of considerations appears to be formally intractable. The computations cannot be done in polynomial time, or as Millgram (2000, p. 87) colorfully puts it, 'there are reasonably sized inputs for which you will not be able to solve the problem—at any rate, not before the universe freezes over'. This means that under these conditions the rationality of a course of action, construed as the best fit of a number of constraints, can never in principle be known if that number is sufficiently large. Given the enormous amount of background knowledge that we bring to any problem, that number of constraints will indeed be large. Clearly, we must find some way of framing problems-solutions so that much of this background does not figure, or better, does not need to figure, in cognitive processing.

From having earlier faintly disparaged toy universes and hinted at the virtues of wielding large coherent conceptual schemes to deal with life's complexities, it is time to champion the virtues of smaller cognitive worlds.

That we can often solve problems, or at least make epistemic progress, by effectively bracketing much background and focusing on just one or two aspects of a situation, is a commonplace. Here is an example of focused trial-and-error learning by a teacher (or actually a group of teachers) that can easily be formulated to fit a simple Popperian schema for the growth of scientific knowledge: $P_1 \Rightarrow TT_1 \Rightarrow EE_1 \Rightarrow P_2$ (Popper, 1979, pp. 164–165; Chitpin & Evers, 2005). Helen is a primary school teacher in Hong Kong and the initial pedagogical problem (labeled P_1) she and her colleagues addressed was how to promote certain generic skills in Primary 3 students through doing project work on famous heritage areas in Hong Kong. For this they formulated an initial tentative theory (TT_1) whose salient feature is expressed by a single hypothesis, with everything else assumed as background. This theory was then acted upon, and difficulties or errors emerged that suggested areas where errors needed to be eliminated (EE_1). The Popper Cycle then repeats with a new problem formulated out of a desire to address the errors, and the original problem. As can be seen from Figure 4, such knowledge building is not guaranteed to terminate at a particular point. But in this case, there is evidence of gains in knowledge.

In asking whether this kind of approach will support claims for the trans-cultural objectivity of small cognitive world problems, it is worth distinguishing two issues. If it makes sense, in this context, to abstract altogether from the question of agreement over background knowledge, so that both problems and solutions can differ for different cultures, then what remains of a common approach to rationality is just the procedural apparatus of securing a best fit of whatever subset of claims is in play. This would be analogous to proposing the trans-cultural validity of a logical argument while waiving consideration of its soundness, or the truth of its premises.

However, if we wish to construe rationality in a broader epistemic sense, such as the sense in which best fit models are used to sustain inferences to the best explanation, or to justify clusters of claims, or to underwrite the sense in which Helen is making epistemic progress, then we need to pursue the possibility of touchstone, or agreed bodies of background knowledge. The central difficulty turns on the fact that, as Fodor (1983, pp. 104–119) puts it, the total body of knowledge that is involved in setting our beliefs is isotropic and Quinean. It's isotropic because evidence or theory that is relevant to the justification of our beliefs can come from anywhere in our system of thought. And it's Quinean because the global properties of the whole system are relevant to the determination of the epistemic value of a piece of evidence. Selecting what knowledge to avoid revising in light of additional evidence is an instance of what is known as the 'frame problem'. (See Dietrich & Fields, 1996.) As the literature on this is both voluminous and mostly unhelpful (but see Shanahan, 1997), I shall focus on just one line of inquiry that seems promising.

In his book, *The View from Nowhere*, Thomas Nagel posits a continuum between subjectivity and objectivity in the following way:

> A view or form of thought is more objective than another if it relies less on the specifics of the individual's makeup and position in the world, or on the character of the particular type of creature he is. The wider the range of subjective types to which a form of understanding is accessible— the less it depends on specific subjective capacities—the more objective it is. (Nagel, 1986, p. 5)

Popper Cycle 1	Popper Cycle 2	Popper Cycle 3	Popper Cycle 4	Popper Cycle 5
P1: How to develop Primary 3 students' generic skills through doing a project on the famous heritage areas in Hong Kong?	P2: How to develop Primary 3 students' generic skills through observation in a site visit for a project?	P3: How can the grading of a worksheet show the level of achievement in each generic skill?	P4: How to decide the assessment rubrics so that the learning performance of students can clearly be shown?	P5: How to improve the revised assessment rubrics for the easy understanding of Primary 3 students?
TT1: This is achieved by arranging site visits.	TT2: This is achieved by using guide questions in a worksheet.	TT3: This is achieved by using assessment rubrics.	TT4: This can be achieved by revising the assessment rubrics with more hierarchical divisions for the next site visit.	
EE1: Feedback from teachers after the decision found that there is a need for helping children gather data and develop necessary generic skills in the site visit.	EE2: Feedback from teachers after marking the worksheet with different grades suggests the need for a clear meaning of the grading for different target generic skills for both teaching and learning purposes.	EE3: Feedback from teachers after marking the worksheet with the initial design of assessment rubrics reveals difficulty in marking with an over simplified assessment rubric mechanism.	EE4: Feedback from students reveals that the revised assessment rubrics are too complex for their understanding.	

Figure 4: Helen's Knowledge Building in a local primary school

Since there's no such thing as a view from nowhere, an alternative task for anyone attempting to defend some account of objectivity is to specify circumstances under which specific subjective capacities and circumstances do not result in a relativity of epistemic judgments. One such attempt at specification is that proposed by Sen (1993, pp. 466–467), where he introduces a further distinction between objectivity that is position-dependent ('positional objectivity') and that which is trans-positional, involving 'synthesizing different views from distinct positions'. Sen explains positional objectivity with the aid of an example: 'The sun and the moon look similar in size'. This claim is position-dependent because to someone on the moon, Neil Armstrong perhaps, the claim would not be true. It would depend on the position of the observer. But if the observer were in a similar position, they would agree with the claim. Hence a claim can be person-invariant and position-dependent, and can enjoy a certain amount of objectivity in that it is relatively independent of the individual, idiosyncratic features of observers.

Unfortunately, this account becomes problematic when, as Sen wishes, we expand the notion of positionality to include additional, non-spatial, parameters that may affect perceptions: living in a particular society, bearing a particular culture, experiencing a particular kind of education. Then it looks like, for example, 'belief in women's inferiority in particular skills' (Sen, 1990, p. 10) enjoys positional objectivity for people in a society where the prevalence of these ideas is an outcome of such positional parameters. Sen (1990, p. 10) attempts to block this conclusion by arguing that there is always the possibility of internal critique, even in that society, and hence the view is non-necessary, and so is not positionally objective. My worry, however, is that if we came into the debate with concerns about culture affecting the objectivity of reason, we'll have much the same concerns over the objectivity of internal critique. Under these circumstances, the view from nowhere is best countered by defending the possibility of a view from everywhere.

Defending the possibility of a view from everywhere amounts to arguing that there is enough common human experience to render plausible the notion of a common, or touchstone, view of reasoning about similar things across cultures. Take, for example, a small cognitive world embedded in the operation of a set of variably linked binary switches. Because this world is so constrained, anyone contemplating and interacting with the setup in its limited pattern of operation should reach the same conclusion about how it might work as a set of logic gates for truth tables, or for adding or multiplying binary numbers. It would be like a jigsaw puzzle, or a set of *su doku* numbers that fit together in a unique way. And its algebraic properties could be extracted and described at the appropriate level of abstraction.

Now consider the case of an initial learner who is interacting with middle-sized dry physical objects. Following Grandy (2006, p. 2) let's propose that these objects satisfy the criterion of '*maximal dynamic cohesiveness*—meaning roughly that moving one part of the object tends to move it all'. More precisely, 'maximal' means that the object is not part of another object, and 'dynamic cohesiveness' means that if a force acts on one part of the object it can be regarded as acting on all of the object. Although examples of these objects will vary from culture to culture, a vast portion of an infant's time will be spent in interaction with elements of this kind.

In common with the binary switches, these elements exhibit a characteristic pattern of behavior in interactions. Take the behavior of a collection of variously shaped blocks of different sizes and place them into groups A, B, C, and so on. Gathering together groups A and B first, and then group C has the same effect on the total number of blocks as gathering together B and C first and then A. This is the associative law of addition. Switching two piles around and adding them has no effect on the total number of blocks either. Hence, addition is commutative. Placing blocks in columns and rows, and interchanging these (simply by rotation or change of viewing perspective) shows that multiplication is commutative. More impressive manipulations will give the associative law of multiplication, and less impressive ones will yield up additive identity, additive inverses and the distributive law.

These characteristic patterns, and others to do with causation and the physics of objects, arguably underwrite patterns in elementary forms of reasoning and logic. (See Halmos, 1962; Halmos & Givant, 1998.) That the infant's arms and hands may also be included among the objects appropriate for such a developing abstract model of the world adds a useful reflexiveness to these thoughts. Just as the cross-cultural studies, considered earlier, pointed to cultural diversity in some cognitive matters, so there is much research in developmental psychology that tends to support the cross-cultural ubiquity of other features of cognition. In a survey of much of the literature, Karmiloff-Smith (1992) gives a variety of examples, including: '[Number] conservation seems to be universal to all societies'; 'Another seemingly universal fact about number ... [is] ... that almost every society invents or uses additive composition operations' (p. 108). In discussing how young children 'come to theorize about the physical world', she posits 'the internal process of representational redescription which abstracts knowledge the child has already gained from interacting with the environment' (p. 78). Recent work on the role of cognitive artifacts in sustaining thought processes in social practices further develops this last point. For example, the widely duplicated invention of money functions as a powerful conceptual tool for integrating a vast and disparate range of goods and services into a common valuation system for calculating and determining commercial exchanges (Fauconnier & Turner, 2002, pp. 201–203). This blend of artifact and cognition for the solution of small-scale practical problems can further be seen in cross-cultural inventions such as sundials, gauges and compasses. The suggestion is that the trans-culturally common patterns inherent in the manipulation of material objects can scaffold upwards into more elaborate artifactually supported shared cognitive processes; measurement apparatus and procedures for determining property boundaries can even develop a conceptual life of their own as geometry.

If this kind of story is approximately true, then not only does it provide the cognitive conditions for a view from everywhere, but it also provides a way of dealing with the frame problem. Experience should be seen as relevant both to the setting of priorities among claims, and the way claims cluster—that is, the weights among them. The fact that our rationality is bounded in the sense of our having limited computational, memory and informational resources means that although in principle our web of belief may be isotropic and Quinean, in practice the cognitive task would begin with the highest priority claims and pursue relevant reasoning along axes determined by the greatest weights. Shanahan (2004, p. 4) avails himself of this sort of solution when he argues that 'the computational theory of mind can be relieved of the frame problem' if the account of rationality on which it depends is 'suitably modified to allow resource-boundedness'.

Problems are thus scaled down and made more tractable by a process of selective attention to a limited number of features perceived to be most relevant. That from culture to culture it is roughly the same background knowledge that is bracketed off as not central with regard to certain particular, small, well-structured problems, is due in part to the common causal genesis of priorities among these claims and the weights that bind the claims together into a structure. Thus, the mathematicians that proved the *Gougu* Theorem would understand Euclid's proof of Pythagoras' Theorem, we may safely assume. And the Korean inventors of the moveable type printing press, whose invention preceded Gutenberg's by 200 years, would have appreciated the nature of the European's problem and his solution. That these and other common patterns of reasoning might be said to have normative value could be argued from the fact that a solution is found, or that all the constraints, in Nickles's sense, are satisfied.

Conclusion

There is much evidence that human reasoning is not normatively appropriate. Many experiments are able to show significant differences between how people actually reason and the correct way of reasoning in those experimental set-ups. However, once we move beyond small scale reasoning experiments, it becomes harder to specify with the same precision what counts as normatively appropriate cognition. In response, some philosophers have argued that when it comes to larger scale reasoning tasks, the concept of reason itself is tied in with the conceptual schemes invoked for these tasks, and that it is a confusion to question the rationality of human cognition under these broader conditions. Against this conclusion, it has been argued that the notion of reason, in both its descriptive and normative dimensions, fragments precisely where larger conceptual schemes reflect significant cultural differences. The objectivity of reason seems therefore to be compromised by there appearing to be culturally relative standards.

Against this line of argument, I have urged that we look for cross-cultural objectivity in reasoning about well-structured, small scale issues and problems, where the normative once again becomes clearer and the computational intractability of the large is not a significant factor. Unfortunately, scaling real problems back down from the richer cognitive contexts in which they are almost always embedded requires dealing with the frame problem; that is, knowing the appropriate body of beliefs to hold constant, or as background. My suggestion was that this knowledge occurs naturally, by dint of the cognitive development of creatures with limited reasoning resources. Furthermore, for some small cognitive tasks, there is cross-cultural evidence that these are seen in much the same way, this time by virtue of the common run of experiences with the world of material objects in early childhood by creatures with similar cognitive endowments. These tasks thus present as similarly structured sets of claims that have similar priority. This is indeed a modest sense of objectivity, but the high level of intercultural articulation that is able to occur among people of different backgrounds suggests that it provides cognitive scaffolding for a lot of other reasoning tasks as well.

References

D'Andrade, R. (1989) Culturally Based Reasoning, in: A. Gellatly, D. Rodgers & J. Sloboda (eds), *Cognition in Social Worlds* (New York, McGraw-Hill).

Chitpin, S. & Evers, C. W. (2005) Teacher Professional Development as KnowledgeBuilding: A Popperian analysis, *Teachers and Teaching: Theory and Practice*, 11:4, pp. 419–433.

Choi, I. & Nisbett, R. E. (1998) Situational Salience and Cultural Differences in the Correspondence Bias and in the Actor-observer Bias, *Personality and Social Psychology Bulletin*, 24, pp. 949–960.

Cohen, J. (1981) Can Human Irrationality be Experimentally Demonstrated?, *Behavioral and Brain Sciences*, 4:3, pp. 317–329, 359–367.

Davidson, D. (1984) *Inquiries into Truth and Interpretation* (Oxford, Clarendon Press).

Dennett, D. (1978) *Brainstorms* (Cambridge, MA, MIT Press).

Dietrich, E. & Fields, C. (1996) The Role of the Frame Problem in Fodor's Modularity Thesis: A case study of rationalist cognitive science, in: K. Ford & Z. W. Pylyshyn (eds), *The Robot's Dilemma Revisited: The frame problem in artificial intelligence* (Norwood, NJ, Ablex), pp. 9–24.

Fauconnier, G. & Turner, M. (2002) *The Way We Think: Conceptual blending and the mind's hidden complexities* (New York, Basic Books).

Fodor, J. (1983) *The Modularity of Mind: An essay on faculty psychology* (Cambridge, MA, MIT Press).

Grandy, R. E. (2006) Soft Borders, Bright Colors: The cognition and metaphysics of everyday objects, http://www.ruf.rice.edu/~rgrandy/Project.pdf

Haig, B. D. (1987) Scientific Problems and the Conduct of Research, *Educational Philosophy and Theory*, 19:2, pp. 22–32.

Halmos, P. (1962) *Algebraic Logic* (New York, Chelsea Publishing Co.).

Halmos, P. & Givant, S. (1998) *Logic as Algebra* (New York, The Mathematical Association of America).

Hutchins, E. (2005) Material Anchors for Conceptual Blends, *Journal of Pragmatics*, 37, pp. 1555–1577.

Karmiloff-Smith, A. (1992) *Beyond Modularity: A developmental perspective on cognitive science* (Cambridge, MA, MIT Press).

Millgram, E. (2000) Coherence: The price of the ticket, *Journal of Philosophy*, 97:2, pp. 82–93.

Nagel, T. (1986) *The View from Nowhere* (Oxford, Oxford University Press).

Needham, J. (1954) *Science and Civilization in China*, Volumes 1–5 (Cambridge, Cambridge University Press).

Nickles, T. (1981) What is a Problem That We May Solve It? *Synthese*, 47, pp. 45–118.

Nisbett, R. E., Peng, K., Choi, I. & Norenzayan, A. (2001) Culture and Systems of Thought: Holistic versus analytic cognition, *Psychological Review*, 108:2, pp. 291–310.

Open Peer Commentary, (1981) *Behavioral and Brain Sciences*, 4:3, pp. 331–359.

Popper, K. R. (1957) *The Logic of Scientific Discovery* (London, Hutchinson).

Popper, K. R. (1979) *Objective Knowledge* (Oxford, Oxford University Press).

Quine, V. W. O. (1960) *Word and Object* (Cambridge, MA, MIT Press).

Samuels, R. & Stich, S. (2004) Rationality and Psychology, in: A. R. Mele & P. Rawling (eds), *The Oxford Handbook of Rationality* (Oxford, Oxford University Press), pp. 279–300.

Sen, A. (1990) Objectivity and Position: Assessment of health and well-being, http://www.grhf.harvard.edu/HUpapers/90_01.pdf.

Sen, A. (1993) Positional objectivity, *Philosophy and Public Affairs*, 22, pp. 126–145. Cited as reprinted in Sen, A. (2003) *Rationality and Freedom* (Cambridge, MA, Harvard University Press), pp. 463–483.

Shanahan, M. (1997) *Solving the Frame Problem: A mathematical investigation of the common sense law of inertia* (Cambridge, MA, MIT Press).

Shanahan, M. (2004) The Frame Problem, *Stanford Encyclopedia of Philosophy*. http://plato. stanford.edu/entries/frame-problem/

Simon, H. A. (1977) *Models of Discovery* (Dordrecht, Reidel).

Stich, S. (1990) *The Fragmentation of Reason* (Cambridge, MA, MIT Press).

Thagard, P. (1992) *Conceptual Revolutions* (Princeton, Princeton University Press).

Thagard, P. & Millgram, E. (1995) Inference to the Best Plan: A coherence theory of decision, in: A. Ram & D. B. Leake (eds), *Goal-Driven Learning* (Cambridge, MA, MIT Press), pp. 439–454.

Thagard, P. & Verbeurgt, K. (1998) Coherence as Constraint Satisfaction, *Cognitive Science*, 22:1, pp. 1–24.

Tversky, A. & Kahneman, D. (1982) Judgments of and by Representativeness, in: D. Kahneman, P. Slovic & A. Tversky (eds), *Judgment Under Uncertainty: Heuristics and biases* (Cambridge, Cambridge University Press).

Wason, P. C. (1966) Reasoning, in: B. Foss (ed.), *New Horizons in Psychology* (London, Penguin Books).

Wong, K. C. (2001) Culture and Educational Leadership, in: K. C. Wong & C. W. Evers (eds), *Leadership for Quality Schooling: International Perspectives* (London, Routledge/Falmer), pp. 36–53.

Wu, W. (1983) Out-in Complementary Principle, in: Y. Mao (ed.), *Ancient China's Technology and Science* (Beijing, Foreign Language Press).

4

Is There a Geography of Thought for East-West Differences? Why or why not?

HO MUN CHAN & HEKTOR K. T. YAN
City University of Hong Kong

Nisbett's *The Geography of Thought* (2003) is one of several recent works that have highlighted purported differences in thinking patterns between East Asians and Westerners on the basis of empirical findings; it has implications for teaching and other issues such as cultural integration. This paper offers a critical examination from a philosophical perspective of Nisbett's view on these apparent differences in ways of thinking, with particular attention given to the alleged differences in relation to critical thinking. In the following section we outline a naturalistic approach to the study of human rationality. Based on this approach, the notions of ideal rationality, adaptive rationality and critical rationality are developed. In the third section a geography of thinking styles that is different from Nisbett's is constructed by applying the three notions of rationality. In the fourth section we reject Nisbett's claim that East Asians have a stronger tendency to think 'illogically' than do Westerners. In the fifth section, we argue that Nisbett's geography of thought is inaccurate because the alleged differences between Eastern and Western styles of thinking are not real or overstated, and suggest that our geography of thought can provide a more adequate account of thinking styles across cultures. In the final section, implications for the teaching and learning of critical thinking are drawn from the geography we develop in this paper.

A Naturalistic Account of Human Rationality

Norms of rational belief are one of the major concerns of epistemology, philosophy of science, and philosophy of logic. Philosophers in these areas have attempted to develop theories that can serve both as guides to and as codifications of good reasoning strategies and practices. Over the past two decades there have been rapid developments in the psychology of human reasoning and in the analysis of computational complexity. These developments have led to dissatisfaction with some philosophical theories of reasoning, for example, formal theories of logic and probability, based on the following two criticisms. First, the argument from complexity, to the effect that these theories are often so idealized that no ordinary people would be able to fully follow many of the norms proposed. This criticism originates from mathematical findings in complexity analysis, results of research conducted by researchers in the field of Artificial Intelligence (AI) (e.g. Herbert Simons, 1972, 1983), psychologists (e.g. John Anderson, 1990, 1991), and philosophers (e.g. Christopher Cherniak, 1984, 1986). Second, the argument from irrationality, to the effect that if these theories serve to define human rationality, then human beings must be inherently irrational because many psychological experiments have shown that there is a general human tendency to deviate from the norms proposed by these theories. This criticism stems from the experimental work of psychologists, including Johnson-Laird (1983), Daniel Kahneman, Paul Slovic, and Amos Tversky (1982). These theories are said, in other words, to prescribe norms for godlike beings or perfectly rational agents: hence we might call them theories of *ideal* rationality.

An adequate theory of human rationality should obviously not be a theory of ideal rationality. It should aim to stipulate norms that are attainable by earthly beings. In order to construct such a theory, philosophers need to take seriously findings in the history of science, psychology, and other disciplines in cognitive science: hence the rise of a naturalistic approach to the problem of human rationality. A central thesis of such an approach is that a normative model of human reasoning and action cannot be properly constructed without taking seriously facts about biology, psychology, and social and cultural conditions of human beings. The approach does not aim to make philosophy a chapter of psychology, because philosophy is undeniably concerned with norms of rational belief rather than the description of epistemic performance. However, a normative account of human reasoning needs to take seriously the two criticisms above, i.e. the argument from complexity and the argument from irrationality. The norms of rational belief need to be identified in the context of a set of background empirical theories that characterize the capacity of the human mind, the ecological structure of the environment, and the goals of reasoning activities. Although people often use reasoning strategies that deviate from the norms stipulated by theories of ideal rationality, many of the strategies are heuristics that enable cognitive agents with limited power to achieve their cognitive goals in their living environments at a low computational cost (Funder, 1987; Anderson, 1990, 1991; Gigerenzer, 1991, 1998; Kornblith, 1993; Cosmides and Tooby, 1996).

The above account does not imply that formal theories of logic, probability, decision analysis, and so on, are insignificant in the study of reasoning. The principles of these theories are often not the normative principles used by humans in their daily reasoning; they might rather serve as background theories and provide a set of mathematical tools for *vindicating* the heuristics of human rationality. Together with the background empirical theories, these formal theories can be used to show that the heuristics of human rationality enable human beings with limited cognitive power to maintain their survival in their normal living environments effectively, though these heuristics may lead humans astray in some unusual situations. In other words, these formal theories can help us demonstrate that the heuristics of human rationality work reasonably, though not perfectly, well in our daily lives, and that we have to live with the imperfection given that our cognitive capacity is limited.

A good example to illustrate the above point is the availability heuristic. Our estimation of the likelihood of an event often depends upon how easily we can imagine examples of the same event. The availability of an example to the mind depends upon how recent, how familiar, or how salient the example is: the more so in each case, the stronger and more unreflective the psychological tendency to follow the heuristic. A number of experiments seem to have shown that the availability heuristic often leads us astray. Yet these experimental results are misleading. Theories of probability can be used to show that if we take into account the relevance of different kinds of information in our environments (e.g. more recent information is more likely to be important), the heuristic actually enables us to retrieve useful information quite quickly with a reasonable level of accuracy (Anderson, 1990, 1991). People are more likely to make these errors when they are placed in experimental settings different from their usual environments (Anderson, 1990, 1991; Lopes & Oden, 1991). So it can be shown mathematically that the heuristic can help humans cope with problems arising from their living environments quite effectively, though not perfectly.

The earlier literature to do with bias in the use of heuristics gives a pessimistic picture, that human reasoning is systematically irrational and that people often have a strong tendency to make obvious logical mistakes. One of the well-known findings is that people are likely to follow the Law of Small Numbers by jumping to a conclusion from a small sample (Tversky & Kahneman, 1971; Nisbett & Ross, 1980). However, although the law is not statistically sound, it could be a useful reasoning strategy in an environment where there are regularities and clustering features (Kornblith, 1993). Suppose there is an urn containing 90% white balls and 10% black ones. If in the process of counting them I were to predict that the next ball will be white, I will of course be right 90% of the time. If I were to pull a single sample out, put it back, and predict that the colour of the next ball will be the same as the sample, my chances of being right are $(0.9 \times 0.9) + (0.1 \times 0.1)$ = 0.82. The difference is not very large, but the computational cost is significantly lower than the cost of following the Law of Large Numbers. So the application of the Law of Small Numbers in some specific situations could indeed be vindicated by the formal theory of probability. Further, there is evidence that people are sensitive to what features of objects are likely to be tied together or form clusters: the law is thus very useful in situations where there are clustering features. If we saw a single platypus laying eggs, we would believe that all platypuses lay eggs. The Law of Small Numbers works well as far as such features are concerned. Yet after seeing a single black book, most will not conclude that all books are black. Most are aware that the law is not applicable in all situations.

According to the naturalistic approach to the study of human reasoning, an adequate theory of human rationality is an abstraction of successful epistemic strategies from unsuccessful ones, which consists of a mutual adjustment, or the so-called reflective equilibrium process (Goodman, 1983) between principles of reasoning and successful inferential practices. The adjustment process aims at constructing a coherent set of norms to capture a maximal set of inferential practices that can promote the satisfaction of inferential goals (Thagard, 1988) (see Figure 1).

The process involves using background theories to vindicate that the norms generated are attainable by human agents and can work reasonably, though not

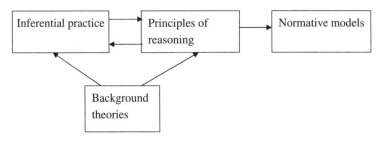

Figure 1: Reflective equilibrium in naturalized epistemology (adapted from Thagard, 1988, p. 128)

Figure 2: Wason's selection task

perfectly, well in the satisfaction of inferential goals in the usual environment. The process is *critical* rather than descriptive because it serves to identify the conditions in which a set of epistemic strategies works well and those in which the strategies fail. It is also *ecological* because the structure of the usual environment and the limits of human cognition are taken into account in the evaluation of epistemic strategies.

Based on this naturalistic account of human reasoning, we can introduce two more notions of rationality in addition to ideal rationality:

> Adaptive Rationality: Human beings are rational in the adaptive sense because they are equipped with reasoning strategies that enable them to achieve many fundamental cognitive goals in their natural and social environments even though their cognitive capacity is limited. The use of these strategies is often spontaneous, unreflective, and largely unconscious. They are built into the human mind by evolutionary forces or acquired through socialization.

> Critical Rationality: A cognitive agent is critically rational if s/he is able to assess the applicability and the limit of his/her adaptive strategies. The naturalistic approach to the problem of rationality is not a purely academic project. Its findings can enhance people's critical rationality by letting them know when their adaptive thinking works and when it doesn't.

With respect to adaptive rationality, psychological studies are useful for identifying the reasoning strategies that people adopt at the adaptive levels. In Wason's (1968) well-known Selection Task, subjects were presented with four cards showing the characters A, D, 4, and 7 (see Figure 2).

Subjects were told that each card has a letter on one side and a number on the other, and that the rule 'If a card has vowel, then it also has an even number' applies to all four cards. Subjects were asked to turn over only those cards that one needs to determine whether the rule is true or false. Most subjects mistakenly

| Drinking Beer | Drinking Coke | 25 years old | 16 years old |

Figure 3: The drinking problem

selected only A, or A and 4. This provides evidence that human beings are weak at applying abstract logical principles in solving unfamiliar problems. Later studies show that a selection task with familiar thematic content can facilitate good reasoning. For example, performance is much better if subjects are presented with the following cards and are asked to assume the role of a police officer in detecting whether anyone has violated the rule 'If a person is drinking beer, then that person must be over 20 years old' (Cosmides, 1989; Gigerenzer & Hug, 1992) (see Figure 3). It seems that humans are equipped with mechanisms to solve specific reasoning problems, such as cheater detection, that loom large in their daily lives.

For quite some time, many psychologists and philosophers understood the early results of Wason's test to provide evidence that human beings are largely irrational or often fail to reason logically even in obvious cases. This misinterpretation of the findings overlooks a fundamental trade-off between tractability and applicability (Levesque & Brachman, 1985), an important result that is well known in the literature of AI, theoretical computer science, and computational informatics. Many cognitive tasks are computationally complex, and the usual trick for a cognitive mechanism to overcome the problem of intractability is to specialize itself in solving the sub-tasks that are crucial for the survival of the cognitive agent. The trade-off is that the cognitive mechanism will work poorly in a domain that lies outside its range of applicability.

A familiar illustration of this is the human visual system. It would be ideal if humans could have a visual system that worked in all possible environments, but many perceptual processes, such as stereopsis (the process by which we perceive depth or distance), are hugely complex, while the computational capacity of our cognitive system is limited. Evolutionary forces drive the visual system to specialize in coping with problems arising from the usual environment. As the work of David Marr has shown (1982), one of the assumptions that the stereopsis mechanism of the human visual system has taken for granted is that surfaces are smooth. Such assumptions can greatly reduce the complexity of stereopsis but the trade-off for the efficiency gain is that the visual system performs poorly in an environment full of things like 'a swarm of gnats [or] a snow storm' (Roth & Frisby, 1986). Further, since identifying three dimensional objects, boundaries and edges is crucial for our survival, as a trade-off our eyes are not very good at perceiving the world as consisting of patches of colours and shadows, a skill that an artist is able to acquire only after special training. The same trade-off can explain many visual illusions in unusual environments or experimental settings.

On more detailed analysis, it can be recognized that the logical problem of solving the abstract version of Wason's Selection Task is rather complicated

(O'Brien, 1993). The task is by no means a simple application of *modus ponens* (affirming the antecedent). It has to be solved in quite a number of steps, requiring the skill of instantiating the variables of a formal rule, a knowledge of *modus tollens* (denying the consequent), which is a more difficult rule of inference than *modus ponens*, and a skilful application of the *reductio ad absurdum*, which is not an easy proof strategy. So a failure to perform the abstract version of the selection task gives no strong evidence that people fail to reason logically even in obvious cases. Furthermore, despite the difficulty, it is not the case that people often perform the task poorly. The drinking problem demonstrates that performance is not too bad when people are asked to cope with logical problems arising in contexts that occur commonly in their daily lives.

The principle of charity provides a further philosophical argument for why it could not be the case that people often fail to reason logically in obvious cases (Quine, 1970; Davidson, 1973, 1976, 1985; Dennett, 1981, 1982; Stalnaker, 1984). According to the principle, an agent cannot be said to have the intentional states ascribed if the content of these states violates the rules of reasoning in obvious cases. (These rules are not necessarily logical rules in the narrow sense: they also include basic rules in probabilistic reasoning and decision-making.) We could hardly make sense of the sentences uttered by the agent because a contradiction would result from such a violation. As Wittgenstein points out, a contradiction is senseless (1961, 1983), and the utterances that sound obviously illogical are a kind of logical 'insanity' or 'madness' (1983).

Some philosophers (e.g. Stich, 1990) and psychologists (e.g. Stanovich, 1999) allege that the principle of charity implies that human agents are ideally rational. This, according to Quine, Davidson and Dennett, is a misreading: they assert that we should preserve the logically obvious in the ascription of intentional states. There are many consequences that intentional agents are not able to derive from the beliefs they hold because of the computational complexity of logical reasoning. Yet in order to explain their behaviour, we may sometimes need to ascribe a belief that is inconsistent with some of those consequences. Furthermore, the principle of charity does not imply that human beings never violate the rules of reasoning in obvious cases either. Human reasoning mechanisms may be disturbed by intervening factors, such as shift of attention, absent-mindedness, or distraction, yet that is not a failure in reasoning and nor is it a fault of the reasoning mechanism itself (Dennett, 1982). The mechanism does not have a built-in tendency to deviate from the fundamental rules of logic in the performance of simple reasoning tasks. So unless a cognitive agent is in an abnormal condition, the ascription of intentional states has to preserve the logically obvious.

Geography of Thought: A Tale of Two Versions

Now, based on the naturalistic account of adaptive rationality developed in the last section, we can derive a geography of thought across different cultures.

First, the thinking patterns of people across different cultures do not contravene the fundamental principles of reasoning in the performance of simple reasoning tasks—otherwise we would not be able to make sense of their thoughts. This is where we have serious disagreements with Nisbett's conclusion that Eastern people have a tendency to think 'illogically' in an obvious way while Westerners don't. This point we elaborate in the next section.

Second, human beings are not ideally rational in the sense that they are not very good at applying fundamental principles of logic to solve non-obvious reasoning tasks. In order to overcome the problem of the computational complexity that comes with ideal rationality, people in different cultures or environments would develop domain-specific strategies to cope with problems that are crucial to their survival or that occur commonly in their daily lives. Tractability is gained at the expense of limiting the applicability of the reasoning strategies developed, and errors are likely to occur when people apply the strategies beyond their ranges of applicability.

Third, there will be some similarities in the natural and social environments of different cultural communities, so it is probable that at the adaptive level people across different cultures will have some strategies in common. Over the past few years, we have informally replicated a number of experiments in our classes, including the selection task and others developed by researchers in the heuristics and biases tradition. We have found that college students and schoolteachers have a strong tendency to follow similar heuristics and make similar mistakes as subjects in the West. They have a similar tendency to follow the availability and represent-ativeness heuristics, manifest similar biases associated with the misuses of these heuristics, have a similar tendency to be misled by the framing effect, make similar errors in the abstract versions of the selection task, and so on. In sum, we find quite a number of similarities at the adaptive level. In his earlier work, Nisbett was a follower of the heuristics and biases approach, and appeared convinced that people across different cultures follow similar heuristics and manifest similar biases in their daily lives. He and Ross produced a book on *human* inference (Nisbett & Ross, 1980). It is with some irony that he has recently moved towards the opposite pole in claiming that East-West differences are fundamental.

Fourth, while the natural and social environments of some cultural communities may be similar in some aspects, and while people in these communities may have adopted some common reasoning strategies at the adaptive level, they have not been universally adopted across all cultures.

Finally, the natural and social environments of each cultural community will also have distinct features, so people in each community may also have unique strategies at the adaptive level.

Figures 4 and 5 are graphical representations of our version and of Nisbett's version of the geography of thought. According to Nisbett's geography, since East-ern styles of thinking tends to be 'illogical' even in obvious cases, it follows that the thinking strategy of East Asians would lie entirely outside the domain of ideal rationality. In contrast, Westerners are alleged to have a tendency to think logically. So in his geography of thought, the patterns of thought in the East and West look entirely separate from one another. We believe that his geography seriously mis-represents any East-West differences in thinking style. So to answer the question that we raised in the title of our paper, if a geography of thought means a geography of

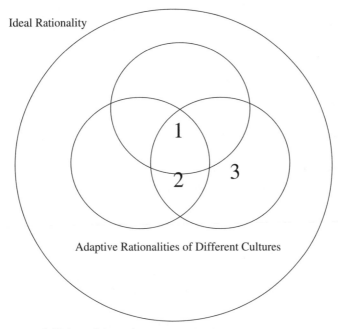

1. Universal reasoning patterns.
2. Patterns shared by some but not all cultures.
3. Patterns unique to a single culture.

Figure 4: The geography of thought: Chan & Yan

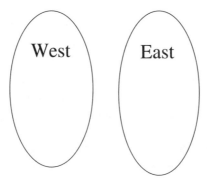

Figure 5: The geography of thought: Nisbett

differences in Nisbett's sense, it does not exist, and if it means a geography of similarities and differences as portrayed in Figure 4, it does.

Nisbett on Logic and Contradiction

A. East-West Differences in Logical (Deductive) Reasoning

Nisbett's arguments to the effect that East Asians are less logical than Westerners are based on experiments about participants' reactions to deductive arguments. He cites three such experiments: in two of the three cases East Asians and Westerners are given examples of deductive arguments and asked to assess how convincing or logically valid they are.

Example 1.1

1. All birds have ulnar arteries.
    Therefore all eagles have ulnar arteries.
2. All birds have ulnar arteries.
    Therefore all penguins have ulnar arteries.

Example 1.2

Premise 1:   No police dogs are old.
Premise 2:   Some highly trained dogs are old.
Conclusion: Some highly trained dogs are not police dogs.

Premise 1:   All things that are made from plants are good for health.
Premise 2:   Cigarettes are things that are made from plants.
Conclusion: Cigarettes are good for health.

Premise 1:   No A are B.
Premise 2:   Some C are B.
Conclusion: Some C are not A.

In another case participants are asked to make logical inferences based on a number of propositions. In all cases it appears that East Asians do not perform as well as Westerners, as they are more easily affected by the plausibility of the premises and conclusions.

Nisbett argues that the difference in experimental outcome could not be the result of a lack of formal training in logic because Americans and Koreans show equal weaknesses when dealing with purely abstract syllogisms in the controlled case. He attributes the difference to the lack of habit on the Koreans' part to apply logical rules to ordinary events.

There are a few points to note concerning these sorts of experiment. First, the experiments highlight an apparent difference in the pre-reflective judgement of logical problems between Westerners and East Asians. That is to say, Westerners perform better than East Asians even before either group have been given training in formal logic. Nisbett concludes from this that East Asians are less used to applying logical rules to everyday situations than Westerners. There is surely no natural or biological difference between Westerners and East Asians that could account for this fact. Exposure to deductive (logical) reasoning is hard to measure: people use logical rules of inference in their everyday life when most are unaware of this fact. This implies that all people have some intuitive grasp of logical inference. (It is inconceivable for anyone *not* to have used a *modus ponens* inference in everyday life.) From this it follows that training in formal logic is nothing more than a further refinement or development of something people already know. Or, we may say that we all have some understanding of the principles of logic so the difference is only a matter of degree. If this were the case, then it would make no sense to say that participants from a Western or East Asian background are *not* trained in formal logic.

Second, the experimenters appear not to have given due consideration to the normative nature of logical thinking. Nisbett hinted at the 'illogical' tendencies of East Asians, and the implications of the difference in habits between Westerners and East Asians remain to be seen. From the perspective of teaching logic, the difference in cultural habits does not affect the nature of logical thinking as a normative activity. This is to say, what counts as logically valid or invalid has its own criteria, and such criteria remain independent of people's actual habits or even their preferences. The role of an educator would therefore hardly be challenged: to enable the students to *become* competent in logical thinking.

Third, it is worth pointing out that assessing arguments from a logical perspective in terms of validity or soundness is actually technically demanding. Grasping the notion of validity, which is an essential notion in deductive reasoning, requires the ability to think at a high level of abstraction. In other words, to master logical reasoning one needs to evaluate an argument purely in terms of its formal structure: its actual factual content, no matter how ridiculous or counterintuitive it may appear, must be ignored. Since logical validity is of such a nature, it is counterintuitive to one not trained in formal logic. When asked to evaluate an argument, it is unlikely that an ordinary person will distinguish the validity of an argument from the empirical truth of its premises from the soundness of its conclusion. This implies that an ordinary person would tend not to distinguish the formal from the non-formal properties of an argument. Thompson (1996) asked participants to judge the 'acceptability' (in an ordinary, non-technical sense of the word) of arguments: results show that their judgements are affected by both the logical validity *and* the factual content of the arguments. What is significant about this Thompson's study in relation to this discussion is that the experiment was conducted on Western subjects. Failure to distinguish logical validity and factual content in an argument is a cross-cultural phenomenon. This does not rule out the possibility that once people are given enough formal training, they are as likely to form good logical judgements, no matter whether they are of Western or Eastern origin.

B. Attitudes Towards Fundamental Logical Principles

Having claimed that East Asians are apparently less used to applying logic in their everyday lives than Westerners, Nisbett then goes on to discuss a more fundamental difference in thought between Westerners and East Asians: their attitudes towards contradictions (Nisbett, 2003, pp. 173ff). Western and Eastern participants in an experiment were asked to state their preferences with respect two different sets of proverbs:

Half a loaf is better than none.
One against all is certain to fall.
'For example' is no proof.

Too humble is half-proud.
Beware of your friends, not your enemies.
A man is stronger than iron and weaker than a fly.

Nisbett finds that East Asians have a stronger preference for the second set of proverbs, and believes that such differences can be traced back to a style of 'reasoning' that can be called dialectical. He describes this style as characterized by an absence of 'hard and fast rules', and claims that it can be further characterized as involving three principles: the Principle of Change, the Principle of Contradiction and the Principle of Relationship, or Holism. Nisbett points out that the three principles that underlie dialecticism conflict directly with some fundamental logical principles such as the law of identity and the law of non-contradiction.

To simplify the discussion, we will concentrate on the law of non-contradiction. What is important with respect to Nisbett's argument is that the law of non-contradiction is often considered fundamental to human thought. In other words, it is believed that without such a law, thought and communication would become impossible. Now if it is indeed the case that East Asians have a thinking style that violates the law of non-contradiction, it can no longer be considered to be fundamental because it is no longer universal. This also implies a disturbing form of cultural relativism. Huss (2004) argues convincingly that dialecticism and East Asians' attitudes towards apparent contradictions do not show that East Asian thinking violates the law of non-contradiction. Without repeating Huss' arguments, we may still examine Nisbett's experiments and their implications in a relatively simple manner.

To begin with, let us consider dialecticism in relation to the notion of context. Aristotle explicitly stated that the law of non-contradiction is *not* a context-free claim: 'the same attribute cannot at the same time belong and not belong to the same subject in the same respect' (*Metaphysics*, 1005b19–20).[1] To see whether dialecticism violates the law of non-contradiction, it is necessary to understand what dialecticism means within specific contexts. In addition, if we are concerned with clarity, we ought to point out that dialecticism often involves ambiguity.[2] For example, the statement, 'Wealth means poverty is around the corner' (Nisbett, 2003, p. 177), can mean the following:

1. The presence of wealth indicates that poverty is imminent.
2. The presence of wealth makes it easier for people to become aware of the existence of poverty.

Once the ambiguity is pointed out, it becomes obvious that an apparently contradictory claim is not contradictory in any logical sense, for none of the interpretations of the statements involves any logical inconsistency: the first interpretation suggests a usual (or unusual) sequence of events while the second one states a fairly common psychological phenomenon, namely the fact that wealth and poverty are relative notions depending on how people compare themselves with one another. It is not the case that wealth is taken to mean *non*-wealth. Viewed from this perspective, dialecticism is not in direct conflict with fundamental logical laws such as identity or non-contradiction (or the excluded middle).

In the following experiment Nisbett has, in our view, been insufficiently cautious in interpreting the results. Chinese and American graduate students are given stories about interpersonal and intrapersonal conflicts due to diverging interests or impulses. They are then asked to analyse the stories and (presumably) suggest some way to resolve them. Nisbett and Peng (his co-researcher) then categorize the resolutions as dialectical (or Middle Way) or non-dialectical. 'A dialectical response usually included sentences that attributed the cause of the problem to both sides and attempted to reconcile opposing views by compromise or transcendence. ... Non-dialectical responses generally found exclusive fault with one side or the other' (2003, pp. 177–8). The results clearly indicate a Chinese preference for dialectical responses and an American preference for non-dialectical (one-sided) responses.

Caution is needed in interpreting the result of this experiment. If it shows anything about a difference between Westerners and East Asians, what exactly is it about? One may think that since dialecticism is based on three principles that are in conflict with certain fundamental logical laws, the preference for giving a dialectical response on the part of East Asians could actually show that they are 'non-logical'. However, we should remember that the experiment is about stories related to interpersonal relationships and intrapersonal conflicts. It thus demonstrates differences in people's ways of dealing with conflict. In this sense the experiment's findings concern the participants' attitudes towards social relationships or personal choice; it is only remotely related to logic.[3]

At this point, we should make clear our view that Nisbett fails to restrict his use of the word 'contradiction' to its literal, logical meaning. Putting aside the question whether Nisbett interprets Aristotle appropriately, it is certainly the case that his use of 'contradiction' is ambiguous. First, for Nisbett, a 'contradiction' can refer to a statement which suggests the coexistence of contrary or contradictory ideas or qualities. However, we have seen that there is no real contradiction involved in this sort of statement because the presence of *linguistic* ambiguity is the cause of this illusion. Second, the preference for some sort of compromise when dealing with a situation where *conflicting* views or demands are present is misinterpreted by Nisbett as an example of accepting 'apparent contradiction' (2003, pp. 183–4).

This misinterpretation can be found in another experimental study conducted by Peng and Nisbett. In the experiment, subjects are shown two opposing statements (but not contradictory in the logical sense) that are unlikely to be true at the same time. Nisbett provides two examples (2003, pp. 181–182):

Example One:

Statement A: A survey found that older inmates are more likely to be ones who are serving long sentences because they have committed severely violent crimes. The authors concluded that they should be held in prison even in the case of a prison population crisis.

Statement B: A report on the prison overcrowding issue suggests that older inmates are less likely to commit new crimes. Therefore, if there is a prison population crisis, they should be released first.

Example Two:

Statement A: A social psychologist studied young adults and asserted that those who feel close to their families have more satisfying social relationships.

Statement B: A developmental psychologist studied adolescent children and asserted that those children who were less dependent on their parents and had weaker family ties were generally more mature.

From Nisbett's description, this is how we understand this experiment was conducted. There are two groups of subjects, one Chinese and one American. Each group is further divided into two sub-groups. One of the Chinese subgroups and one of the American subgroups are given only one statement from each pair of statements and are asked to rate their plausibility. Nisbett could thus ascertain how plausible each single statement appeared to the Chinese and the Americans. The next step of the experiment involves the remaining two subgroups. Instead of being given one single statement, they are presented with the pair of statements and they are again asked to rate their plausibility. The results show that when Chinese subjects are given a pair of statements, the rating of the more plausible one goes down while that of the less plausible one goes up. The American response is the opposite when they are given a pair statements—the more plausible looks more so and the less looks less so. Nisbett concludes that this can be explained by the Chinese' feeling it 'necessary to find the truth in each of two contradictory propositions' (2003, p. 182). The American's reaction, Nisbett added, shows their preference for generating counterarguments. As Nisbett says, 'when confronted with a weak argument against a proposition they are inclined to believe, they have no trouble in shooting it down' (2003, p. 183).

Before discussing the implications of this experiment, we should first clarify an important point: since none of the examples is contradictory in the logical sense, Nisbett's conclusion that the experiment can show something about the subjects' attitudes towards contradiction is probably unsubstantiated. However, the results of the experiment do show some difference between Westerners and East Asians: they do have opposing tendencies in dealing with statements that *seem* contradictory or *seem* to be in conflict. How are we to make sense of this?

Two different issues are present here. First, are the responses given by the Chinese and the Americans who are presented with pairs of statements appropriate? Second, if there is indeed this difference in their responses, what does it imply? Concerning the first, Nisbett comments that the responses of the Chinese and the Americans are both inappropriate. However, this view lacks justification because the two subgroups who gave different ratings are not composed of the same subjects; as a result, they cannot properly be charged with inconsistency. So, the only issue concerns the significance of the difference between Chinese and American responses when both groups are given pairs of statements to rate.

Here we propose that the differences indicate the presence of two different adaptive rational strategies. The Chinese tendency to rate two apparent 'contradictions' in a less polarizing fashion than Americans might tend to serves a practical function, namely, the avoidance of direct confrontation or the prevention of disgrace for people who hold to the less plausible statement. The American tendency, though different from the Chinese tendency, is not without practical function either. The readiness to produce counterexamples implies the likelihood of claims being refuted—this is an essential part of the process where more substantial and accurate claims replace less substantial and less accurate claims. In other words, this attitude might be seen as a crucial component of scientific progress. Having said that, it does not follow that the Chinese response is less logical or illogical. The rival statements in the experiment are contraries, not contradictory. The law of non-contradiction is not violated if someone asserts that they are both false, because the truth may lie in the middle. This can be used to explain the different responses of the Chinese participants. When both statements are shown to them, the Chinese participants may be more likely to think that the truth lies in the middle. And, if the middle point is used as the reference, the more plausible statement will look less so while the less one will look more so.

To see the differences between Americans and East Asians as different expressions of adaptive rationality can also be applied to another experiment discussed in Nisbett's book. Here American and East Asian subjects are asked to give reasons for their choice of objects such as a computer when presented with three options.

> When asked to justify their choices, Americans moved to a preference for one of the extreme objects whose choice could be justified with reference to a simple rule, whereas Asian participants moved to a greater preference for the compromise object. Participants gave justifications that were consistent with their choices: Americans were more likely to give rule-based justifications and Chinese were more likely to give compromise-based justifications. (Nisbett, 2003, p. 184)

Contrary to Nisbett's view, this shows little about the East Asians' disregard for real (logical) contradictions. Rather, it indicates a significant difference in the *preferences* of Westerners and East Asians. In short, our central position still holds: there are still important and fundamental ways of thinking shared by Westerners and East Asians, to which Nisbett gives insufficient credence.

Although Nisbett fails in our view to establish the conclusion that East Asians are in any way 'non-logical', the experimental findings discussed in his book do indicate some differences in tendencies.[4] If it is appropriate to characterize such differences as different adaptive rationalities, the difference does not imply a violation of the law of non-contradiction in East Asian styles of thinking.

We might point out that East Asians do not deny the law of non-contradiction in the logical or Aristotelian sense. Aristotle has offered some insights concerning the fundamental nature of the law of non-contradiction.[5] As we mentioned earlier, for Aristotle the acceptance of the law of non-contradiction is *not* purely an abstract issue: he reminds us that in the context of actual discourse or argument, the denial of the law of non-contradiction would lead to two possibilities: either it is the case that one can no longer say anything meaningful (for to say '*p* and not-*p*' would put any listener into confusion) or one must remain silent. A similar point is also made by Wittgenstein (1961, 1983). In other words, the law of non-contradiction is part of our *practical* life, so it remains to be shown that it can be intelligibly violated. In addition to this response, we ought to bear in mind that an apparent contradiction resulting from linguistic ambiguity is no real contradiction, and the mere *preference* for compromise is a practical strategy, which may have ethical or social significance but as such has little relevance to basic logical principles.

Nisbett mentions that there are only two short-lived movements in logical inquiry in the East. However, it obviously remains true that East Asians can master logical reasoning. The fact that East Asians tend to be less familiar with abstract, logical reasoning does *not* show that East Asians have a different logic or logical system. To give a more comprehensive picture of Eastern intellectual history, we ought to point out that examples of logical arguments that aim at exposing logical contradiction or inconsistency are actually abundant even outside the Logical and Mohist school—some Legalist and Confucian thinkers are competent in logical reasoning. Dialecticism remains an interesting phenomenon, but, as we have argued, it does not contradict fundamental logical principles. More importantly, it does not seem to have direct relevance to the kind of logical thinking that is taught under the heading 'deductive reasoning/argument' in critical thinking courses.

Nisbett eventually moves to the conclusion that Asians are 'non-logical' (2003, p. 188). We might sum up his main points about East Asian thinking styles as follows:

1. The presence of 'Eastern' dialecticism;
2. The preference to reach a compromise instead of to create a confrontation;
3. The preference to focus on divergent aspects of *apparently* contradictory statements in order to avoid confrontation; and,
4. The preference willingly to interpret statements in order to dissolve apparent contradictions.

None of these shows that East Asians are 'non-logical': the alleged East-West difference is thus not real. Nisbett points out that East Asians do not have trouble with formal logic, although they are 'less likely to use it in everyday situations where experience or desire conflicts with it'. From this observation he seems to have drawn the wrong conclusion that 'East Asians and Westerners differ in fundamental assumptions about the nature of the world ... , in the inclination to use rules, including the rules of formal logic'. He later entertains the possibility that 'there are cultures that don't reason as "we" do' (2003, p. 202).[6] As we have tried to show, this is not true as far as logicality is concerned.

How Radical are East-West Differences in Thinking Style?

We have argued that the differences in thinking style identified by Nisbett fail to support his provocative claim that East Asians are 'non-logical'. His account of the differences is problematic also because they are exaggerated for the following two reasons.

First, the so-called 'Eastern' style of thinking can also be found in the thinking patterns of Westerners. Proverbs that look contradictory are not rare in the West.[7] 'With friends like X, who needs enemies?' sounds very much like a Western counterpart of 'Beware of your friends, not your enemies'[8] or 'Keep your friends close; keep your enemies even closer' (*The Godfather*).[9] The Chinese proverb 'Too humble is half proud' sounds close to what is known as 'false modesty' in the West.[10] So there is also the presence of dialecticism in Western styles of thinking. In another study by Peng and Nisbett, Chinese and American students were presented with both 'logical' and 'dialectical' arguments to prove the existence of God (2003, pp. 181–182). The results of this study seem to suggest that Chinese students are more likely to be convinced by dialectical arguments than American students. The First Cause argument is used as a representative of the 'logical' argument type. However, as Huss points out, many formulations of the argument, including Peng and Nisbett's version, contain the premise that nothing can exist without a cause and the conclusion that something must exist in itself: the conclusion thus 'comes dangerously close to contradicting' the premise (Huss, 2004). The so-called 'dialectical' argument clearly does not, however, violate the law of non-contradiction. As Huss points out, it is a Berkeley-type argument which claims that people can see things only from different perspectives, which implies that they cannot see the whole truth; yet the 'ultimate truth' must exist and be known, and since only God can know it, God must exist. Although American students are more likely to be persuaded by the First Cause argument, they seem, at least in this case, to be more dialectical than Chinese students.

Second, the differences identified by Nisbett are often differences in degree rather than in kind. His discussion about categorization illustrates this well. Based on the experimental evidence that East Asians tend to make judgements of similarity more on family resemblance than rules, Nisbett writes:

> If the natural way of organizing the world for Westerners is to do so in terms of categories and the rules that define them, then we might expect that Westerner's perceptions of similarity between objects would be heavily influenced by the degree to which the objects can be categorized by applying a set of rules. But if categories are less salient to East Asians, then we might expect that their perceptions of similarity would be based more on the family resemblance among objects. (Nisbett, 2003, pp. 141–142)

Categorization is conceived as a process of applying rules to features. For example, mammals are regarded as animals that nurse their young. The rule-based model is only one model of categorization. It should be pointed out that ancient Confucian philosophers already had the idea of 'rectifying names', which means the clarification of ambiguous concepts by giving clear definitions. From this we can see that the rule-based model is not entirely foreign to East Asians. At the same time, the idea of family resemblance is not entirely Eastern either. In Western philosophy, Wittgenstein (1967) is a well-known champion of the idea that concept words (e.g. 'game') are meant to mark the family resemblance between things that they label. Perceiving similarity between objects in terms of family resemblance does not imply a failure to organize the world in terms of categories. Nisbett mistakenly assumes that categorization must be rule-based, but the model of family resemblance is another model of categorization in Western psychology (Medin & Rips, 2005). Perhaps there is evidence that East Asians are more likely to organize the world in terms of family resemblance, but such a style of thinking is also common in Western culture. Commonalities between the East and the West should not be overlooked: what is identified here is only that different cultures place different emphases on the two strategies.

Though the East-West differences are not as radical and fundamental as Nisbett claims, he has indeed identified some interesting differences between East Asian and Western styles of thinking. Yet these are differences at the adaptive level that can be evaluated at the critical level. Some of his findings show that East Asians seem more capable of recognizing an object in terms of its relation to its context and to other objects, while Westerners seem more capable of recognizing an object in terms of its individual qualities. For example, Chinese people make finer cate-gorical conceptualizations of distance in human relationships, reflected in their language: people are not just grandparents, parents, uncles and aunts, nephews and nieces, and cousins—distinctions are made between paternal and maternal grand-parents, and paternal ones are perceived as more proximal. The finer taxonomy of human relationship may enhance the mastery of relational logic, a topic that an introductory course of elementary logic at the college level may not cover because of its level of difficulty. Yet it does not imply that Eastern styles of reasoning are always superior. In a world where objects have stable links with their environments and other objects, Eastern styles of thinking may be more efficient for object recognition, but might perform poorly in a world where objects have high mobility. So there are different trade-offs between tractability and applicability for the two different styles of thoughts.

We have indicated that differences in attitude towards rival claims can also be explained socially. Chinese people might be more in favour of striking a compromise in order to maintain harmonious relations. Choosing the middle way or following the mean is a thinking strategy that is adaptive to a social environment which treasures harmony. From a logical point of view, this thinking style, as we have argued, is no less logical than that of the American subjects in Nisbett's experiment.

Some Implications for the Education of Critical Thinking

Finally, our geography of thought developed in this paper also has important implications for the teaching and learning of critical thinking. In a critical thinking course, it is very common that students are taught to apply a set of fundamental principles of logic and to avoid falling into the traps of a number of fallacious or biased patterns of thinking. A common phenomenon is that the complexity involved in putting logical reasoning *into practice* has often been neglected and students often find it difficult to apply the fundamental principles in their academic work and daily lives. If teachers had a better understanding of the adaptive character of human reasoning, they would appreciate that students' logical reasoning also has to be trained in a domain-specific or context-sensitive way. In other words, we should remind ourselves that the ability to reason needs to be developed and that it takes time for students to master this ability: merely learning the abstract principles has only a limited effect in improving students' ability to deal with thinking problems in different contexts. Another common shortfall in the teaching of critical thinking is that after learning how to identify fallacies and biases in human reasoning in a critical thinking course, many students have a tendency to over-generalize and mechanically apply what they have learned. As we have discussed in this paper, while many non-logical patterns of reasoning are adaptive strategies, errors occur when they are applied beyond the ranges of their applicability. From this we can see that what is needed is *not* some extra abstract principles. Instead, we should accept the fact that people have to make judgments from time to time and a good thinker is a person who makes appropriate judgments in particular circumstances.

To conclude, we need to bear in mind that good thinking needs to be developed or learned through different stages. Logic or reasoning (or critical thinking) is not something homogeneous: there are different ways or forms of reasoning, and they are often adaptive strategies in response to particular problems in human life. If students are taught to be more aware of the natural and cultural contexts in which their thinking patterns are embedded, they should become more sensitive to their own ways of thinking and less likely to misapply them or make hasty judgements based on them.

Acknowledgements

We are much indebted to Laurence Goldstein and Philip J. Ivanhoe for their comments and suggestions. They are of course not responsible for any mistakes in this essay.

Notes

1. Cf. Plato's view in *Republic*, Book IV, 436b: 'Clearly one and the same thing cannot act or be affected in opposite ways at the same time in the same part of it and in relation to the same object; so if we find these contradictions, we shall know we are dealing with more than one faculty' (translation by Desmond Lee). Understood thus, Aristotle's or Plato's view on contradiction would see an apparently contradictory claim, such as Heraclitus' statement that one can and cannot step into the same river, as involving no real contradiction.
2. In the same text (*Metaphysics*), Aristotle provides a clue as to how one should deal with apparent contradictions: he states: 'it will not be possible for the same thing to be and not to be, except in virtue of an *ambiguity*, just as one whom we call "man", others might call "non-man"' (1006b, 18–20, translation by Ross, italics added).
3. This raises another more complicated question: How ready are the participants to *reinterpret* the propositions to dissolve the apparent conflicts? One may say that a charitable reinterpretation expands one's perspective so that different positions can *coexist* harmoniously. By contrast, the identification of an actual contradiction can facilitate *elimination* or *falsification*.

This is in agreement with Wittgenstein's position: not only is it the case that different *games* seem to be present here. It also suggests that what is tested (or what is meant) with an experiment is never self-evident: cultural expectations or agreement in judgements is crucial in deciding *how* a person is meant to react to an experiment. In other words, it is not clear whether Western and Eastern participants in the type of experiments discussed in Nisbett's book share enough agreement before they actually disagree on certain views.

4. Another experiment (2003, pp. 186–7) examines the reaction of participants to statements that are 'literal or near-literal opposites of each other'. It shows that Koreans tend towards agreement while Americans tend towards disagreement. Although this does not clearly indicate any difference in the participants' attitude towards basic logical principles, it does reveal another difference in preference, which can be understood as a difference in adaptive rationality. Alternatively, one might see the differences between Koreans and Americans as different *interpretive* strategies: Americans are more *focused* on the same aspects of the statements, which means that they are more likely to see the contradictory sense of the statements. Koreans, by contrast, divert their attention so confrontations are avoided. A further way to reinterpret this phenomenon is as follows: The East Asians' concern with compromise or harmony can actually be seen as a *reaction* to the reality or possibility of conflict or confrontation in real life. From this we may claim that despite their preference for certain compromising strategies, the East Asians' ability to recognise potential conflict is as acute as the Westerners'.

5. *Metaphysics*, Book IV, Section 4.

6. Nisbett here quotes Stephen Stich, who wrote: 'this makes a shambles of the reflective equilibrium principle. If people don't agree about whether an inference is justified or not, we can't use the principle as a guide to correct thinking—just an expression of personal preference' (2003, p. 202).

7. We owe this point to Laurence Goldstein.

8. We owe this example to Laurence Goldstein.

9. We owe this example to Philip J. Ivanhoe.

10. We owe this point to Laurence Goldstein.

References

Anderson, J. R. (1990) Is Human Cognition Adaptive? *Brain and Behavioral Sciences*, 14, pp. 471–485.

Anderson, J. R. (1991) *The Adaptive Character of Thought* (Hillsdale, NJ, Lawrence Erlbaum Associates).

Aristotle (1984) *The Complete Works of Aristotle: The revised Oxford translation*, two vols., ed. J. Barnes (Princeton, NJ, Princeton University Press).

Cherniak, C. (1984) Computational Complexity and the Universal Acceptance of Logic. Reprinted in H. Kornblith, *Naturalizing Epistemology*, 2nd edn. (Cambridge, MA, MIT Press, 1993) pp. 239–261.

Cherniak, C. (1986) *Minimal Rationality* (Cambridge, MA, MIT Press).

Cosmides, L. (1989) The Logic of Social Exchange: Has natural selection shaped how humans reason? Studies with Wason selection task. *Cognition*, 31, pp. 187–276.

Cosmides, L. & Tooby, J. (1996) 'Are Humans Good Intuitive Statisticians After All? Rethinking some conclusions from the literature on judgment under uncertainty.' *Cognition*, pp. 1–73.

Davidson, D. (1973) Radical Interpretation. Reprinted in D. Davidson, *Inquiry into Truth and Interpretation* (Oxford, Clarendon Press, 1984) pp. 125–140.

Davidson, D. (1976) 'Hempel on Explaining Action.' Reprinted in D. Davidson, *Actions and Events* (Oxford, Clarendon Press, 1980) pp. 261–276.

Davidson, D. (1985) Replies to Essays, in: B. Vermazen and M. Hintikka (eds), *Essays on Davidson: Actions and events* (Oxford, Clarendon Press) pp. 242–252.

Dennett, D. C. (1981) True Believers. Reprinted in D. C. Dennett, *Brainstorms* (Brighton, UK, Harvester Press, 1978) pp. 13–36.

Dennett, D. C. (1982) Making Sense of Ourselves. Reprinted in D. C. Dennett, *The Intentional Stance* (Cambridge, MA, MIT Press, 1987) pp. 83–102.

Funder, D. C. (1987) Errors and Mistakes: Evaluating the accuracy of social judgment, *Psychological Bulletin*, 101, pp. 75–90.

Gigerenzer, G. (1991) On Cognitive Illusions and Rationality, *Pozanan Studies in the Philosophy of the Sciences and the Humanities*, 21, pp. 225–249.

Gigerenzer, G. (1998) The Modularity of Social Intelligence, in: A. Whiten and R. Byrne (eds), *Machiavellian Intelligence II* (Cambridge, Cambridge University Press).

Gigerenzer, G. & Hug, K. (1992) Domain-Specific Reasoning: Social contracts, cheating, and perspective change, *Cognition*, 43, pp. 127–171.

Goodman, N. (1983) *Fact, Fiction, and Forecast*, 4th edn. (Cambridge, MA, Harvard University Press).

Huss, B. (2004) Cultural Differences and the Law of Noncontradiction: Some criteria for further research, *Philosophical Psychology*, 17:3, pp. 375–89.

Johnson-Laird, P. N. (1983) *Mental Models* (Cambridge, Cambridge University Press).

Kahneman, D., Slovic, P. & Tversky, A. (eds) (1982) *Judgement under Uncertainty: Heruistics and biases* (Cambridge, Cambridge University Press).

Kahneman, D. & Tversky, A. (1972) Subjective Probability: A judgment of representativeness, *Cognitive Psychology*, 3, pp. 430–454.

Kornblith, H. (1993) *Inductive Inference and Its Natural Ground: An essay in naturalistic epistemology* (Cambridge, MA, MIT Press).

Levesque, H. J. & Brachman, R. J. (1985) A Fundamental Tradeoff in Knowledge Representation and Reasoning. Reprinted in R. J. Brachman and H. J. Levesque (eds), *Readings in Knowledge Representation* (Los Altos, CA, Morgan Kaufmann) pp. 42–70.

Lopes, L. L. & Oden, G. C. (1991) The Rationality of Intelligence, *Poznan Studies in the Philosophy of the Sciences and Humanities*, 21, pp. 199–223.

Marr, D. (1982) *Vision* (San Francisco, Freeman).

Medin, D. L. & Rips, L. J. (2005) Concepts and Categories: Memory, meaning, and metaphysics, in: K. J. Holyoak and R. G. Morrison (eds), *The Cambridge Handbook of Thinking and Reasoning* (New York, Cambridge University Press) pp. 37–72.

Nisbett, R. and Ross, L. (1980) *Human Inferences: Strategies and shortcomings of social judgment* (Englewood Cliffs, NJ, Prentice Hall).

Nisbett, R. E. (2003) *The Geography of Thought: How Asians and Westerners think differently ... and why* (New York, The Free Press).

O'Brien, D. P. (1993) Mental Logic and Human Irrationality: We can put a man on the moon, so why can't we solve those logical-reasoning problems?, in: K. I. Mankelow & D. E. Over (eds), *Rationality: Psychological and philosophical perspectives* (London, Routledge).

Plato (1987) *Plato: The Republic*, trans. D. Lee (Harmondsworth, Penguin).

Quine, W. V. O. (1970) *Philosophy of Logic* (New Delhi, Prentice Hall of India).

Roth, I. & Frisby, J. (1986) *Perception and Representation: A cognitive approach* (Milton Keynes, UK, Open University Press).

Simons, H. A. (1972) Theories of Bounded Rationality, in: C. B. Radner and J. R. Radner (eds), *Decision and Organization* (Amsterdam, North-Holland).

Simons, H. A. (1983) Alternative Visions of Rationality. Reprinted in P. K. Moser (ed.), *Rationality in Action: Contemporary approaches* (Cambridge, Cambridge University Press) pp. 189–206.

Stalnaker, R. C. (1984) *Inquiry* (Cambridge, MA, MIT Press).

Stanovich, K. E. (1999) *Who is Rational? Studies of individual differences in reasoning* (Mahwah, NJ, Lawrence Erlbaum Associates).

Stich, S. (1990) *The Fragmentation of Reasoning* (Cambridge, MA, MIT Press).

Thagard, P. (1988) *Computational Philosophy of Science* (Cambridge, MA, MIT Press).

Thompson, V. A. (1996) Reasoning from False Premises: The role of soundness in making logical deductions, *Canadian Journal of Experimental Psychology*, 50:3, pp. 315–319.

Tversky, A. & Kahneman, D. (1971) Belief in the Law of Small Numbers. Reprinted in Kahneman, Slovic, and Tversky (1982), pp. 23–32.

Wason, P. C. (1968) Reasoning about a Rule, *Quarterly Journal of Experimental Psychology*, 20, pp. 273–281.

Wittgenstein, L. (1961) *Tractatus Logio-Philosophicus*, trans. D. F. Pears & B. McGuiness (London, Routledge and Kegan Paul).

Wittgenstein, L. (1967) *Philosophical Investigations*, eds G. E. M. Anscombe and R. Rhees, trans. G. E. M. Anscombe (Oxford, Basil Blackwell).

Wittgenstein, L. (1983) *Remarks on the Foundations of Mathematics*, eds G. H. von Wright, R. Rhess & G. E. M. Anscombe, trans. G. E. M. Anscombe (Cambridge, MA, MIT Press).

5

False Dichotomy? 'Western' and 'Confucian' concepts of scholarship and learning

JANETTE RYAN & KAM LOUIE
Monash University, Australia; The University of Hong Kong

A critical juncture currently exists for both Western and Asian higher education systems due to the increased transnational flow of academics and students between Anglophone universities and their Asian counterparts. This interflow should provide new ways of knowing, making meaning and interacting for those within these systems. Yet, too often, this has not been the case. Discourses of internationalisation of higher education often position Western and Asian education systems and scholarship in terms of binary opposites such as 'deep/surface', 'adversarial/harmonious' and 'independent/dependent', and uncritically attribute these labels to whole populations and communities of practice.

Such approaches frequently rely on 'ideal' models that do not take into account the diversity and complexity of the contemporary social and cultural situatedness of such practices, nor of how they are played out within individual contexts. Some of the basic tenets, or 'ideals', that are held up as the virtues of these systems need to be deconstructed in the context of both Anglophone and Asian realities so that their effectiveness can be assessed. Only then can a genuine dialogue be established between (and within) these systems. We need to explore the possibilities for a new way forward that works from an understanding of these complexities and a genuine attempt to learn from the unfamiliar 'other'. This stance requires as its precursor an examination of whether the usual characterisations of 'Western' and 'Asian' academic values are useful, accurate or valid.

Too often, 'Western' and 'Asian' values are characterised as discrete, homogenous and unchanging. This point was illustrated in the Call for Papers for the Philosophy of Education Society of Australasia's 34th annual conference, *Critical Thinking and Learning: Values, concepts and issues*, in November 2005:

> Education in the different countries of Australasia and Asia is informed
> by widely differing historical and cultural perspectives, from western to
> Confucian, from liberal to communitarian, from colonial to postcolonial.
> Hong Kong, in many ways, lies at the crossroads of many of these
> perspectives. To what extent, for example, are the dominant concepts of

thinking and learning a product of 'western' cultural values? Might they be in conflict with concepts and values said to be prevalent in many Confucian-heritage cultures that apparently stress the meditative mind, harmony of thought and harmony in relationships, filial piety and a tempered questioning of authority, and the transmission of received wisdom through time? Might the liberal ideal of the independent and autonomous individual clash with communitarian values of identity in relationship?

Although clearly intended to prompt discussion, this excerpt (deliberately) draws on the binary logic often found in the literature describing Chinese education and Western education as exclusive and definable.

In this article, we explore assumptions and characterisations such as this. To focus the task more clearly, we will use the perceived Confucian-Western dichotomy as a case study and Australia as the site on which these 'values' are played out. Australia is a perfect case for study because it has been the site of intense negotiations between different cultural values in recent years.

Asian Students in Changing Australian Educational Contexts

Dramatic changes in cultural values have been most keenly felt in higher education in Australia, partly due to the influx of 'international students'. For example, in 2004, 24.2 percent of all students (nearly one in four) were international students, the highest level of any OECD country, with the vast majority of these students coming from Asian countries such as China, Singapore, Malaysia and Indonesia (DEET, 2005). While many in the higher education sector have expressed reservations about this turn of events, more outward-looking academics and the Australian government welcome this trend. The former see the internationalisation of higher education bringing different and new approaches to learning while the latter sees it as good business. Certainly, international education comprises 15 percent of Australian university revenue and is an AUD 6 billion industry (DEST, 2004).

Unfortunately, the rapid expansion of the university sector in Australia has meant that government funding in proportion to the number of students has declined, so despite the income generated by international students, many academics in Australian universities report rapidly deteriorating professional conditions such as increased workloads, bigger class sizes and diminished research funding. Some associate the worsening conditions with the increased student intake from overseas. The lack of training in teaching students from different cultural backgrounds has not helped matters, and lecturers understandably often feel that the demands placed on them are unreasonable (Ryan, 2002). Such radical changes in workload and the types of issues confronting academics sometimes mean that their reactions are negative and hostile. Papastephanou (2005) characterises these responses as 'antagonistic impulses cultivated by globalisation' (p. 533). The consequent 'intellectual and emotional significance' of globalisation needs to be debated, Papastephanou argues, to inform the 'direction globalization and the theorisation of the cosmopolitan pedagogical ideal must take' (p. 534).

Ritualistic responses or 'antagonistic impulses' characterise much of the literature surrounding the increase in the numbers of international students in Anglophone countries. The discourses of globalisation, played out in higher education as attempts to 'internationalise' the curriculum, rarely involve an examination of the appropriateness of conventional Western pedagogical approaches to contemporary, more globalised and culturally interdependent contexts for both domestic and international students. The more common response is token efforts that merely provide 'add-ons' such as the inclusion of international examples to university curricula (Webb, 2005). As Webb points out, internationalisation must move beyond such superficial approaches:

> The idea of internationalisation of curriculum is more radical and refers to the integration of a global perspective to curriculum development. This means that content does not arise out of a single cultural base but engages with global plurality in terms of sources of knowledge. (Webb, 2005, p. 110)

Despite the now significant numbers of students from countries with Confucian-heritage cultures (CHC) studying in Australian universities, and the increased academic 'flow' between the CHC countries and Australia in these spheres, many misunderstandings and negative stereotypes abound about international students from Asian countries. These construct Asian or CHC students as having outlooks that are opposites of Western academic values, and many construct 'deficit' views of them as learners (Fox, 1996; Ryan, 2002), viewing them in terms of the characteristics that they lack, rather than those which they bring to their new learning environments. Thus, CHC students are often characterised as passive, dependent, surface/rote learners prone to plagiarism and lacking critical thinking.

These characteristics are then represented as the antithesis of Western exemplars of academic virtue. Such characterisations are so powerful that CHC students often internalise these constructions themselves, describing themselves as 'passive' and accepting this as a negative attribute. This is despite their previous academic achievements in their home countries, and the fact that international students achieve similar rates of academic success as domestic students in their higher education studies in Australia (DEST, 2004). Such official figures belie the charge of 'decline of academic standards', soft marking and rampant plagiarism, clearly seen in the 'misconceived and ill-targeted' debate over academic standards (De Vos, 2003). The tensions surfacing in such debates may also arise from the resistance by academics to the increased expectations of commercialisation and entrepreneurialism in their work (DeVos, 2003) occurring in parallel with the increases in the numbers of international students. Their frustrations are often directed at those who represent the physical manifestation of these changes.

Equally, well-intentioned but ill-informed attitudes towards CHC students can have negative consequences for international students. Piecemeal or naive attempts to gain cultural knowledge about their international students by Western academics can be based on stereotyped, outdated and inappropriate views of the 'Asian learner' or indeed of 'Asians' in general (Louie, 2005). One example of such well-intentioned advice comes from a newsletter distributed by the James Cook University Academic Support Division. Based on readings of research conducted by authorities such as Watkins and Biggs (1996, 2001), the author Gina Curro provides very good summaries of current research debunking myths such as claims that CHC students are passive and surface learners. However, Curro's enthusiasm leads to inaccuracies. Thus, in her attempts to refute the common perception that Chinese students are highly competitive, she states that 'the ancient Chinese proverb, "Friendship first, competition second", refutes this myth'. Curro contends that 'Chinese socialisation practice emphasises sharing, cooperation and acceptance of social obligations, and it de-emphasises competition and aggression'. These sentiments are generous and welcome as counterbalances to academic misunderstandings of CHC students as having cultural 'deficits'. However, by over-correcting a misperception, Curro herself falls into the same trap of homogenising and thus misinterpreting a cultural tradition that is as complex and diverse as any other.

The CHC Student: From Deficit to Surplus Value

In fact, Curro's description of Chinese culture is misleading. The maxim 'friendship first, competition second' is not an ancient Chinese proverb. It is a recent piece of propaganda that gained wide currency, especially during the early 1970s, when China had few friends in the world and was desperately trying to win some by 'ping-pong diplomacy'. China won most of the matches anyway, and losing a few table-tennis games was in reality part of the strategy to compete for 'friendship'. Like everyone else, some Chinese are very testosterone-driven while some are more inclined to have 'feminine' interests. Curro is clearly misinformed about ancient Chinese notions of sport and friendship, and in turn, she misleads. However one defines Chinese culture, one can be sure that for the Chinese athletes training for the 2008 Olympics, competition is uppermost in their minds. If the common perception that Chinese students are very competitive in Australia is false, it is worth pointing out that it is doubly mistaken to imply from this false perception that Chinese students everywhere are competitive or that Chinese culture is competitive. However, it is also a mistake to go to the other extreme and claim that Chinese culture values friendship above competition. Counteracting a 'deficit' theory with a 'surplus' theory is understandable, but it is not helpful.

Such 'surplus' interpretations of CHC students by the well meaning are not difficult to make, given that what are considered Chinese beliefs span a huge spectrum of differing and contradictory ideas and patterns of thought. We will shortly return to look at how the Chinese in Mainland China have radically changed their assessments of Confucian education. For the moment, it is worth considering the most prevalent interpretations of the 'Confucian' in CHC. This has become a key term for investigation since the explosion, to which we have alluded, of 'international students' in Western countries. When Anglophone universities such as those in Australia found it difficult to handle the influx of the newly coined CHC students, educationalists such as Ballard and Clanchy (1997) sought ways to help their 'deficit' students by characterising them in ways that the 'Asian values' promoters in the 1980s and early 1990s have characterised 'Asian values': namely, that Asian (specifically Confucian) education promoted communitarian values, respect for knowledge and tradition. However, these values are of course not just Asian: they can be found in other societies as well. While some good work was done in this area, the so-called 'Asian values' or 'Confucian heritage' could be devised by putting together conservative ideas and calling them Asian and Confucian. Many people—often theorists who had little direct experience in teaching in Asia, particularly the 'Confucian' countries themselves—did just that. They relied on what the 'New Confucianists' living outside China, such as the influential Columbia University emeritus William de Bary and Harvard-based Tu Weiming, told them about the 'communitarianism' of Confucianism and neo-Confucianism (de Bary, 1998; Tu, 1996).

By the late 1990s, some educationalists researching and teaching in Asian countries were trying to redress the 'deficit' theories with a more positive spin on CHC students' learning behaviour. In advocating the 'surplus' learning perspective mentioned above, Curro specifically acknowledges that even the title of her newsletter, *Teaching the Chinese Learner*, is based on the books *The Chinese Learner: Cultural, psychological and contextual influences* (1996) and *Teaching the Chinese Learner: Psychological and pedagogical perspectives* (2001), edited by the (then) two University of Hong Kong educationalists David Watkins and John Biggs. Chapter Two of the 1996 book, on conceptions of learning in Confucianism, is in fact written by Lee Wing On, who was also at The University of Hong Kong at the time.

Lee Wing On, like other educationalists well disposed towards CHC students, begins his chapter with the assertion that 'Asian students are not only diligent, but they also have high achievement motivation. Invariably they have a high regard for education'. He 'aims to uncover what underlies Asian people's positive attitude towards education, their achievement motivations, and their willingness to spend most of their free time in pursuit of study' (Lee, 1996, p. 25). Lee believes, as do many other commentators, that the answer to this quest lies in Confucianism, which is explained by him as the belief in educability and perfectibility for all, learning for self-improvement, and so on. While Lee is aware that elaborating Confucian ideas of education as explanations of the Asian students' love for learning may lead to over-generalisations, he assumes with conviction but no proof or argumentation that CHC students 'invariably have a high regard for education'.

That generalisation is highly questionable, to say the least. We have taught hundreds of Asian students, and some of them do indeed have a high regard for education. But many don't. If teachers begin their classes assuming that their CHC students respect education, what are they to think when a particular Singaporean student enjoys computer games but hates books, or a Hong Kong student loves to party instead of solving mathematical problems? Not only can one be wrong about one's students from another culture, but more importantly, the stereotyping of that culture can also mislead one into classroom interactions that are just culturally inappropriate. Thus, using Lee's essay as an example again, we find that he cites ideas from classical philosophers such as Mencius and Xunzi as well as contemporary thinkers such as neo-Confucianist Tu Weiming and William de Bary to substantiate his claim that Confucian education stands for self-cultivation, egalitarian ideals, reflective thinking and so on. These are people who live thousands of years and thousands of miles apart. Their contexts cannot be more different. Yet, Lee, as most scholars who write on this topic, treats Confucian education for the last two thousand years as a philosophy that remains more or less the same. This is similar to treating Christianity as the same in all places and times.

It is not difficult for teachers to see that their own countries have changed dramatically in the last two or three decades. But many do not see (not having lived there) how even more dramatically East Asian countries have changed. Every few years, these countries physically change almost beyond recognition, so much so that even the superficial physical transformations have many of their own citizens feeling dazed and lost in the new landscape. Social and cultural transformations are occurring at an even more profound level and rapid rate. Mostly they have a Confucian heritage, yes, but that heritage is becoming increasingly difficult to define as perceptions of its nature change with changing circumstances. Similarly, many of us living in countries that profess to be Christian know that the Seventh Day Adventists, Mormons, Quakers and Ku Klux Klan represent very different (and non-Mainstream) brands of Christianity. Apart from the adherents to these sects, nobody would believe that any one of them is the only true Christianity. Yet, in the classroom, difference is most visible by their extreme representations, as the common perception of Muslims as Islamic fundamentalists shows. In the same way, East Asian students are, thanks in no small part to the writings of neo-Confucian philosophers, often seen in stereotypical ways such as having respect for learning and having filial feelings for the teacher (Louie, 2005).

The CHC Student and 'Deep Learning'

As shown elsewhere (Louie, 1986; Louie, 2002, pp. 42–57), in the last century interpretations of Confucianism, particularly of Confucian education, have undergone transformations that have at times rendered any commonly accepted interpretation meaningless. And we should also remember that 'commonly accepted' could mean an interpretation embraced by traditional Chinese scholars, Communist cadres or Western liberal Sinologists. By the same token, what are seen as stereotypes are only characterisations belonging to certain groups of people in specific times and places. Thus, while self-cultivation towards moral superiority is accepted as a major tenet of Confucian education by neo-Confucianists, many influential scholars are now reinterpreting Confucian education as a path to wealth and democracy. Such a view would have been considered outrageous heresy by any traditional Confucian. It is clear that like other great figures such as Christ and the Buddha, Confucius' thinking could be twisted to suit just about all times and needs. Thus, on page 34 of Lee Wing On's paper, John Biggs is cited as arguing that Confucius saw himself as a deep learner. The idea that Confucianism encourages deep teaching and learning processes is in fact the most interesting and perhaps not 'commonly accepted' view in Lee's essay.

This idea is based on Biggs's observation that CHC students are 'deep' learners rather than surface learners. He traces this learning approach back to the teachings of Confucius. Lee makes use of the important and influential work of people like Biggs who challenge the long-held Western belief that CHC learners are passive, compliant and disposed to rote learning so that their understandings of matters at hand are superficial and mechanical. Such beliefs have been so prevalent and entrenched that even CHC students themselves have often internalised these descriptions of themselves and accept the image of themselves as lacking in initiative, being socially inept and boringly bookish. Western teachers by contrast have also internalised the notion that their own personalities and cultures are assertive, independent-minded and better skilled socially. 'Reality' seems to support this belief because in any society, of course those brought up in that society will operate more skilfully and effectively. And the teachers in general are either in their home societies or control the social norms in the classrooms. But effective social behaviour does not always translate into effective strategies for learning.

Scholars such as Biggs have therefore performed an important and necessary service to the practice of teaching CHC students in debunking the 'deficit' model. However, it should be remembered that while it is refreshing to have the stereotypes of Asian students as ineffective rote learners challenged and negated, we should be cautious that we do not go to the other extreme and see a once maligned educational system as a born-again saviour. That is, Confucianism may not be as reactionary and unsuitable for the modern world as some Chinese radicals have depicted it, but it would not be helpful to see it as straightforwardly superior to modern Western practices: otherwise, we end up with just a reversed form of stereotyping. For example, when Biggs tries to resolve the paradox of 'bad' teaching and learning habits with 'good' results among CHC students, he observes that the students have in fact achieved not a superficial but a deep understanding of problems posed, and he comments that 'one of the reliable outcomes of a deep approach is a correct answer' (Biggs, 1996, p. 45). A correct answer to what?

Of course, if the students' sole aim in their work is to achieve good examination results, and they are dedicated to realising that aim, then they are bound to become skilled in providing 'correct answers' in assessment exercises. But examination success does not always indicate deep understanding of problems posed. The idea that repetition or rote learning could lead to deep learning would be appreciated by anyone who plays sport. Practice makes perfect refers not simply to physical perfection. In Chinese culture, for example, calligraphy and painting are said to lead to enlightenment of the mind, as do the practice of martial arts and other repetitive exercises. It is often said that only when a person has mastered the forms and patterns of given tasks, whether in academic disciplines or martial arts, can a 'deep' understanding of its ultimate goals be achieved. Nonetheless, the point about a 'deep' understanding of these various skills is that ultimately, there is no 'correct' answer as such. This is not a criticism of Biggs, more a query about paradoxes of teaching and learning cultural knowledge (Louie, 2005).

Assumed Values of Western Education

Equally problematic is the stereotyping of 'Western' education across time and space and the characterisation of Western students as assertive and independent, critical thinkers. Western students do not invariably have these attributes of course, and their valorisation can have negative impacts on individuals within this system who do not possess these attributes (assuming we know what they are).

Western, Anglophone universities have espoused such attributes as the natural outcomes of a system that evolved and was well suited to an elite population, and not surprisingly, to Western cultures and societies. However, the impact of increasing massification of higher education in countries like Australia in recent decades and the consequent radical changes in the nature of the student cohort (McInnis, 1998) and the nature of its learning needs (Ryan, 2002) have transformed educational expectations and outcomes. Webb (2005) argues that 'to some extent diversity was masked by a shared language and culture' (p. 113) and these changes have only highlighted many existing tensions and problems. These tensions can surface in debates surrounding the 'internationalisation' of the curriculum, which rarely involves an examination of the appropriateness of teaching and learning practices for contemporary higher education contexts. As DeVos (2003) argues, international education is often simply taken to mean the increased flow and presence of foreign students in industrialised countries like Australia. It seldom takes into account whether either domestic or international students consider their higher education experiences to be well suited to their future, more globalised, working lives. International students themselves often report dissatisfaction with their new university experiences (Ryan, 2002) and an awareness that they are the new 'cash cows' for an economically struggling and squeezed higher education sector.

Like Confucian ones, Western educational values and student attributes cannot easily be defined since they depend in large measure on their social and cultural contexts, and these are constantly changing. Furthermore, these values and attributes are not necessarily unique to such systems. And within 'Western' cultures, there exists a diversity of academic beliefs and values, and abilities. There can be more diversity within educational systems from different academic traditions than between them, such as between colonial and postcolonial systems. A school in India using English as the mode for instruction and modelled in the British tradition, for example, may have more in common with a prestigious English 'public' school than another school in close geographical proximity. The same would be true of schools and universities in some other Asian regions with CHC students such as Hong Kong and Singapore.

Wu (2002), writing about his experiences in England as an international student from Taiwan, found that pedagogical approaches changed markedly when he attended different English universities. He suggests that there are different 'microclimates' of pedagogical ethos within cultures and nations 'which may be more salient than those between them' (p. 387). Even within individual contexts there can be a multiplicity of meanings of pedagogical concepts: critical thinking, deep learning, lifelong and lifewide learning and plagiarism. Yet such terms are often cited to describe the attributes that international students lack. How can academics assess their students on the basis of such notions as critical thinking when they in fact do not share common understandings of them?

The questioning approach underpinning critical thinking is presumed to be unique to Western pedagogy, and is said to have its genesis in the Socratic tradition.

Thus, a more experienced mentor skilfully leads the neophyte towards 'discovering' learning for themselves using language as the 'tool' for developing thinking and reasoning. Such approaches are said to be foundational to Western pedagogical practices and even seen as sacrosanct. But clearly, Socrates was not the only sage who led his students through the dialectical process of questions and more questions. Both the Buddha and Confucius were said to delight in leading their better disciples to enlightenment through a process of questions and answers. In the modern classroom, the pathway to a critical questioning approach is usually characterised and assessed through the verbalization of thought processes, using Vygotskian notions of language as the tool for thought. This view can in some part explain the preference for talk or verbal participation in Western classrooms. Indeed, in some Western university courses, marks are allocated for 'active participation' in tutorials, often characterised by an 'adversarial' or argumentative stance, without necessarily much regard for the quality or appropriateness of such participation.

'Critical Thinking' and Other 'Western' Values

The notion of 'critical thinking', however, is not an uncontested concept, nor are there common understandings amongst academics of what it is. In a study of perceptions of the term by academics in a Business Faculty at a large Australian university, Hang (2005) found a remarkable lack of common understanding of the term; many claimed that although they could not easily define the concept, they 'knew it when they saw it'. In education, there are diverse points of view on how best to define this concept philosophically so that it could be usefully employed. Philosophers of education such as Mark Mason (2000) have attempted to defend an integrated conception of critical thinking by considering the ideas of significant theorists such as Robert Ennis, Richard Paul, John McPeck and Harvey Siegel. Despite such efforts, however, there is currently no agreement among academics about such an apparently pivotal concept. Nonetheless, international students are often judged as lacking this attribute. As Yoshino (2004) points out, this may be due more to a lack of appreciation of different styles of expression:

> It is particularly infuriating to hear problems with such rhetorical styles attributed to imagined inadequacies in the student's education in their home country. I have often had conversations in which it has been suggested to me that Oriental students come from backgrounds in which originality and critical thinking are valued less than acceptance of orthodoxy. Apart from the lack of critical thinking apparent in the use of the category Oriental, such analysis is misleading because it confuses differences in style of expression with a lack of academic rigour. What it fails to understand is that a prizewinning English academic essay translated word for word into Japanese is likely to be received as clumsy and ill thought out. (Yoshino, 2004, p. 10)

Other amorphous terms such as lifelong learning (Candy, 1991) and lifewide learning (ACDE, 2001) are equally slippery. Interpretations of these terms are many and varied, and sometimes very simplistic and under-theorised. They have become fashionable in relatively recent times as desirable educational outcomes in the West but this doesn't necessarily mean that such outcomes are unique to such systems. Lifelong and lifewide learning could easily be said to have parallels with the virtues associated with Confucianism. This is particularly true for those like Lee Wing On who argue that Confucianism has as one of its central educational tenets the belief that learning is for self-improvement throughout life.

Critical thinking, independent learning, lifelong and lifewide learning, and adversarial forms of argument are cited as virtues of Western education and seen as desirable goods available to international students. But this assumes that such attributes are indeed universally desirable and attainable, and unique to and commonplace in Western education. Do these attributes exist more in rhetoric than reality? Many academics marking first and second year students' essays would seriously doubt that these attributes are commonly found amongst Western students, but these 'ideals' are being used to measure the 'success' of international students. Not only may international students lack a grounding in the outward behavioural manifestations of such virtues (such as speaking up in tutorials), but such behaviours for them may be more an indicator of a lack of critical or reflective thought and indeed, such students may be very 'critical' of many aspects of the course. Differences in outward behavioural practices in class exist within groups that come from the same culture as well. For example, the quiet student who has not spoken in class during the semester may be equally capable of achieving a high score for his or her work. Moreover, this student may have a deeper understanding of the issues discussed than the talkative, assertive student.

The expectation of group participation as an end in itself represents something of a paradox. In Western higher education classrooms, group participation is often preferred to more individual or 'passive' classroom behaviours, yet Western educational systems are generally referred to as 'individualistic' in nature, compared with the more 'collectivist' nature of CHC systems. Particular 'virtues' may be more a manifestation of an individual's personality, or social or cultural capital (Bourdieu, 1984), than a demonstration of their learning. Such culturally based assumptions of 'ability' may disadvantage individuals without such behavioural inclinations, regardless of whether they belong to the dominant cultural group or another cultural group, or even gender or social class. Similarly, judgements of individual behaviour based on 'Confucian' views of ability may also advantage or disadvantage individual students. 'Binary' opposites of critical thinking and independent learning, such as harmony and communitarianism, are often heralded as the attributes of CHC students. But such terms are also contested and interpreted differently according to the agendas of those espousing such 'virtues'.

As we indicated above, scholars such as Biggs and Lee have tried to show that the 'deep' approach to learning can be traced back to the teachings of Confucius. The claim that CHC students are 'deep learners' has been used as evidence to debunk the myth that they are superficial, rote learners, as described earlier. Yet, in doing so, many commentators refer to this as the 'paradox' of the Asian learner. The use of the term 'paradox' contains the assumption that Asian students *should not* be able to learn well, even though they do somehow, showing that such commentators still believe Western pedagogical approaches to be superior and only found in Westerners. Equally, a mistaken charge of 'rote' learning could be made against Western scholars who are able to recite the works of great writers such as Shakespeare, an accomplishment not so long ago considered a sign of great intellect and education in Western societies.

Implications for Teachers

Although in this paper we have used the terms Western and Confucian to examine concepts attributed to each of these systems, in reality each comprises complex and diverse systems of cultural practices, often as different from one another in one system as between them. Pedagogical labels can mask the diversity to be found within each system. Rather than taking either a 'deficit' or 'surplus' view of either Western or Confucian education, teachers need to recognise this diversity and complexity within not only other cultures, but their own. Teachers need to become 'anthropologists' of their own culture in order to understand how the normative assumptions underpinning their teaching practices can be problematic for international students or indeed, for other groups of students (Ryan, 2000). Teachers in Australia, for example, may unquestioningly accept pedagogical practices in Australia as the 'norm', but increased flows of people and ideas can provide the stimulus for new ways of thinking and knowing, including about one's self, and a disturbance of binary thinking. According to Kostogriz and Doecke:

> Globalisation has destabilized the normalizing and ordering cultures of modernity by bringing the binaries between self and the Other, between natives and non-natives, into a new kind of spatial relation where the very idea of distance and separation has been replaced by the spatial ontology of proximity, movement and trans-border flows. (Kostogriz & Doecke, 2006, p. 2)

Due to their different perspectives and experiences, outsiders or 'others' often see things that insiders embedded within a culture view as normative and universal. They bring a 'surplus of vision' (Bakhtin, 1990) that helps us to better understand ourselves. 'It is the stranger's Otherness or abnormality that provides a background for norm-defining practices' (Kostogriz & Doecke, 2006, p. 3). Teachers need outsiders such as their international students to act as anthropologists, to take advantage of this 'proximity', in order to learn about their own cultural practices. Thus, the 'interflow' of people and ideas into higher education systems does not need to be a 'problem' to be solved (through the 'adaptation' of teaching practices to suit international students), but rather a source for mutual learning. Kostogriz advocates the construction of a 'thirdspace'—a 'critical pedagogy of space'—that takes into account 'both the multiple and contested nature of learning' and provides for 'intercultural innovations in meaning- and identity- making' (Kostogriz, 2005, p. 203). The debate then shifts from how best to *teach*, to how best to *learn*.

Without this shift, current approaches to pedagogy will probably perpetuate the hegemony of one system of cultural practice over another, and lose opportunities for the development of new knowledge through the critical falsifying of the known.

More importantly, schools and universities in Western countries such as Australia could be radically different in how they approach teaching and learning. We ourselves have taught in different Australian universities, each taking pride in having their own 'cultures' and different 'microclimates' (Wu, 2002, p. 387). And of course, it is well known that within the same universities, the differences between faculties such as Arts and Engineering are tremendous. We must first recognise these differences before discussing 'binaries' between East and West. In teaching our international students, we should remember that, like domestic students, they lead multi-layered lives in which their geographical origin is but one characteristic amongst many. They may have little in common with other international students apart from the fact that they are just that—international students. The heterogeneity of educational systems needs to be recognised as holding 'surprises' or unfamiliar elements for a whole range of students, not just international students.

We have thus attempted to show how characterisations of 'models' and 'virtues' of educational systems are often too generalised to be meaningful. The concrete and practical manifestations of these general paradigms show that they are often less than helpful. Operating in classrooms on the basis of such stereotypes and paradigms can have negative impacts for students, leaving them 'untaught and distraught' (Sanderman-Gay, 1999). Teachers need to avoid both 'surplus' and 'deficit' theories and the 'glorification' of internationalisation, and instead recognise and appreciate complexities both within and between educational systems of practice. The key here is to recognise that simplistic acceptance of stereotypes and generalisations will probably result in 'exotic' or 'tokenist' responses and confusion for teachers about how to respond to the increasing globalisation and internationalisation of the curriculum and their pedagogy (Ryan, 2000; 2005). The 'cosmopolitically sensitive education' advocated by Papastephanou (2005) involves a recognition of complexities and the fostering of mutual understandings to enrich learning. As we have argued elsewhere (Louie, 2005; Ryan, 2005), this entails a meta-cultural awareness and a willingness to meet the learning needs of all students, regardless of their cultural background.

References

Australian Council of Deans of Education (2001) *New Learning: A charter for Australian education* (Canberra, Australian Council of Deans of Education).

Bakhtin, M. (1990) *Art and Answerability* (Austin, TX, University of Texas Press).

Ballard, B. & Clanchy, B. (1997) *Teaching International Students: A brief guide for lecturers and supervisors* (Deakin, ACT, IDP Australia).

Biggs, J. (1996) Western Misperceptions of the Confucian Heritage Learning Culture, in: D. Watson & J. Biggs (eds), *The Chinese Learner: Cultural, psychological and contextual influences* (Hong Kong, Comparative Education Research Centre and Melbourne, The Australian Council for Educational Research Ltd.), pp. 45–67.

Bourdieu, P. (1984) *Distinction: A social critique of judgment of taste* (Cambridge, MA, Harvard University Press).

Candy, P. (1991) *Self-direction for Lifelong Learning: A comprehensive guide to theory and practice* (San Francisco, Jossey Bass).

De Bary, W. T. (1998) *Asian Values and Human Rights: A Confucian communitarian perspective* (Cambridge, MA, Harvard University Press).

Department of Education, Science and Training. (2004) International Higher Education Students: How do they differ from other education students? Strategic Analysis and Evaluation Group Research Note No. 2. Accessed 10 June 2005 at: www.dest.gov.au/research/publications/research_notes/2.htm

Department of Employment, Education and Training. (2005) Selected higher education statistics. Retrieved 2 August 2005 from the World Wide Web at: http://www.dest.gov.au/sectors/higher_education/publications_resources/statistics/default.htm

DeVos, A. (2003) Academic Standards, Internationalisation, and the Discursive Construction of 'The International Student', *Higher Education Research and Development*, 22:2, pp. 155–166.

Fox, C. (1996) Listening to the other. Mapping intercultural communication in postcolonial educational consultancies, in: R. Paulston (ed.), *Social Cartography. Mapping ways of seeing social and educational change* (New York and London, Garland Publishing), pp. 291–306.

Hang, Duong Bich (2005) *Critical Thinking and the Role of Writing in its Development: Perceptions of Faculty of Business staff*. Unpublished Masters Thesis. (Melbourne, Monash University).

Kostogriz, A. (2005) Dialogical Imagination of (Inter)cultural Spaces: Rethinking the semiotic ecology of second language and literacy learning, in: J. Hall, L. Vitanova & L. Marchenkova. (eds), *Dialogue with Bakhtin on Second and Foreign Language Learning* (Mahwah, NJ, Lawrence Erlbaum), pp. 189–210.

Kostogriz, A. & Doecke, B. (2006) *Encounters with 'Strangers': Towards dialogical ethics in English education*. Paper presented at 'The Natives are Restless': Shifting boundaries of language and identity' Conference, Monash University, Clayton, Australia, 3 March 2006.

Lee, W. O. (1996) The Cultural Context for Chinese Learners: Conceptions of learning in the Confucian tradition, in: D. Watkins & J. Biggs (eds), *The Chinese Learner: Cultural, psychological and contextual influences* (Hong Kong, Comparative Education Research Centre and Melbourne, The Australian Council for Educational Research Ltd.).

Louie, K. (1986) *Inheriting Tradition: Interpretations of the classical philosophers in communist China 1949–1966* (Oxford, Oxford University Press).

Louie, K. (2002) *Theorising Chinese Masculinity: Society and gender in China* (Cambridge, Cambridge University Pres).

Louie, K. (2005) Gathering Cultural Knowledge: Useful or use with care?, in: J. Carroll & J. Ryan (eds), *Teaching International Students: Improving learning for all* (London, Routledge Falmer), pp. 17–25.

Mason, M. (2000) Integrated Critical Thinking, *Proceedings of the Thirty-fourth Annual Conference of the Philosophy of Education Society of Great Britain* (Oxford, Philosophy of Education Society of Great Britain).

McInnis, C. (1998) Managing Mainstream and Marginal Responses to Diversity, *Higher Education Management*, 10:1, pp. 29–41.

Papastephanou, M. (2005) Globalisation, Globalism and Cosmopolitanism as an Educational Ideal, *Educational Philosophy and Theory*, 37:4, pp. 533–551.

Ryan, J. (2000) *A Guide to Teaching International Students* (Oxford, Oxford Centre for Staff and Learning Development).

Ryan, J. (2002) *University Education for All: Teaching and learning practices for diverse groups of students*. Unpublished doctoral thesis (Ballarat, University of Ballarat).

Ryan, J. (2005) Improving Teaching and Learning Practices for International Students: Implications for curriculum, pedagogy and assessment, in: J. Carroll & J. Ryan (eds), *Teaching International Students: Improving learning for all* (London, Routledge Falmer), pp. 92–100.

Sanderman-Gay, E. (1999) Supervising Iranian Students: A case study, in: Y. Ryan & O. Zuber-Skerritt (eds), *Supervising Postgraduates from Non-English Speaking Backgrounds* (Buckingham, The Society for Research into Higher Education and Open University Press), pp. 40–47.

Tu Weiming (ed.) (1996) *Confucian Traditions in East Asian Modernity: Moral education and economic culture in Japan and the four mini-dragons* (Cambridge, MA, Harvard University Press).

Watkins, D. & Biggs, J. (eds) (1996) *The Chinese Learner: Cultural, psychological and contextual influences* (Hong Kong, Comparative Education Research Centre and Melbourne, The Australian Council for Educational Research Ltd.).

Watkins, D. & Biggs, J. (2001) (eds) *Teaching the Chinese Learners: Psychological and pedagogical perspectives* (Melbourne / Hong Kong, Australian Council for Educational Research / Comparative Education Research Center).

Webb, G. (2005) Internationalisation of the Curriculum: An institutional approach, in: J. Carroll & J. Ryan (eds), *Teaching International Students: Improving learning for all* (pp. 109–118) (London, Routledge Falmer).

Wu, S. (2002) Filling the Pot or Lighting the Fire? Cultural variations in conceptions of pedagogy, *Teaching in Higher Education*, 7:4, pp. 387–395.

Yoshino, A. (2004) *Well-intentioned Ignorance Characterises British Attitudes to Foreign Students* (The Times Higher Education Supplement, 16 July, p. 18).

6
Learning, Empowerment and Judgement

MICHAEL LUNTLEY
University of Warwick

1.

The idea of learning by training seems straightforward and unproblematic. It is about acquiring habits of mind and behaviour that have been shaped by others. Learning by reasoning is learning in which the pupil works out what to do and what to think for herself. This is a form of mental activity that requires the pupil to think for herself and not just mimic patterns of thought and action proffered by others. We could say she has to exhibit judgement.[1] Because learning by reasoning is based on the pupil working out what to think and what to do, the activity is fundamentally a critical one. Even if the pupil adopts habits of mind and behaviour advocated by others, she does so on the basis of her own assessment. This includes a critical evaluation of the learned activities and some sort of reasoned decision to adopt them, oftentimes to adapt them.[2] In learning by reasoning, the pupil takes some responsibility for what she learns.

In practice, it might be difficult to categorise any given learning activity as definitively either a case of learning by training or learning by reasoning. You might think that most activities include elements of both kinds of learning. Nevertheless, the distinction appears *prima facie* to be well-founded as an analytical tool and it makes sense to test the theoretical adequacy of the distinction as a means of improving our understanding of the concept of learning. Here are two reasons for thinking that the distinction is theoretically well-founded.

First, the distinction demarcates different stages in the learning trajectory of an individual. It can seem natural to think that the earliest stages of learning must comprise predominantly learning by training, with learning by reasoning appearing at later stages of development. Before the pupil can critically appraise her cultural inheritance, she must first learn the practices of reason. The practices of reason must be acquired by training, for otherwise there would be no explanation of how they are acquired other than that the capacity for reasoning is innate. Learning by reasoning requires that the subject already knows how to reason. It cannot therefore be something that is acquired by that form of learning. It must be accumulated through more basic forms of learning, i.e. learning by training.

Second, it seems plausible to hold that learning by training picks out the mode of learning by which pupils acquire the received wisdom of their culture. Learning by training is fundamentally a matter of the transmission of culture including the cognitive, social and political culture. It is a mode of learning in which the pupil is fundamentally receptive. They might acquire habits of action as well as habits of mind, but their attitude to practices of mind and action is basically receptive and uncritical. Practices are not received through the filter of rational scrutiny as in learning by reason. Learning by training is empowering, but only in a limited sense. It empowers the pupil only in so far as it provides the pupil with habits of mind and action that enable her to 'fit in' and be a recognised member of cognitive, cultural and social groups. By fitting in, the pupil is protected from the sceptical scrutiny sometimes afforded to outsiders. Such conformity can offer a limited sense of empowerment that comes from being recognised as a member of the group. In contrast, learning by reasoning facilitates a much more robust sense of empowerment in which the pupil comes to acquire autonomy and responsibility for her behaviour, both mental and social action. The pupil might end up endorsing the habits of the dominant culture but, if so, she does so with deliberative responsibility. This empowerment seems to be much more of an achievement than empowerment by training. It is difficult and it is an achievement that often marks a point of real maturity in the individual's development.

Making some such distinction seems *prima facie* plausible and instructive as an analytical tool for understanding different practices of learning both across cultures and differences of developmental stages within a culture. If learning by training and learning by reasoning are analytically distinct, there can be no argument about the nature of learning as such to say that learning *qua* learning should include both aspects. It would not be a failing in the provision of cognitive development *per se* that an educational system provided only one type of learning, for the two types provide different cognitive achievements. In the absence of a further argument about the desirability of both cognitive achievements being provided, whether or not learning could and should include both aspects would have to be considered in the light of further considerations, e.g. social, cultural and political considerations about the impact of different kinds of learning and different kinds of empowerment upon these wider issues. For example, if you thought that the educational systems of a given culture offered little learning by reasoning, and if that observation were offered as a criticism of that system, it could not be due to a failing to provide learning *per se*. If there were a failure, it would be a failure of the system to serve purposes other than just the purposes of learning.

If the distinction is viable, the question regarding the proper components of learning is not itself a cognitive question. There is one type of learning and empowerment that arises from training and there is the other type that comes from the pupil working out what to think and what to do for herself. What mix of these learning types is best for our educational systems is not a matter to be settled by an account of what is needed for learning to be a cognitive achievement; it is settled by an account of what is needed for learning to play a broader cultural, social or political role. I shall call this the noncognitivist thesis about learning. Noncognitivism about learning requires the distinction between learning by training and learning by reasoning.

I think that the noncognitivist thesis is false, for there is no analytical distinction between learning by training and learning by reasoning. I shall argue that it is central to learning, as a cognitive achievement, that it be learning by reasoning. Human subjects are reasoners. Reasoning and the critical assessment of one's inheritance is not something that has to be learnt. It is not something that follows a more basic learning by training and that is only acquired at later stages in cognitive development. It is something that is central to anything worthy of the name of learning. An educational practice that did not make learning by reasoning central to its activities of learning would be, first and foremost, conceptually flawed and not just culturally, socially or politically flawed. I want to promote a rationalist model of learning by reasoning.

I shall make the case for learning by reasoning by drawing upon Wittgenstein. Wittgenstein's own account of learning is ambiguous. His remarks on the place of training are often read as endorsing a developmental trajectory that starts with learning by training as the basis for later learning by reasoning. In contrast, I want to suggest that key passages in the *Philosophical Investigations* make best sense if you take Wittgenstein to be endorsing a rationalist model of learning. I start with a brief review of the empirical evidence in favour of the rationalist model of learning before turning to the philosophical argument that I take from Wittgenstein.[3]

2.

If the distinction between learning by training and learning by reasoning were well-founded, you would expect it to be operative at the earliest phases of cognitive development, for example, the early stages of language learning. If the distinction were well made, early language learning would be the primary point to identify the trajectory from learning by training to learning by reasoning. The idea that early language learning is learning by training is axiomatic for most philosophers.[4] According to Paul Bloom, however, 'children learn words through the exercise of reason'.[5] Word learning, even at the earliest stages of language acquisition, is a case of learning by reasoning. Bloom has compiled overwhelming empirical evidence for the case for learning by reasoning rather than learning by training at this foundational stage of human cognitive development.[6] This runs counter to the dominant empiricism in philosophical accounts of word learning.

It can seem intuitive that word learning must be a case of learning by training, for language learning surely starts with rudimentary associations of words and objects and the discovery that sounds can produce results. If this were right, early word learning would involve experiencing associations between words and objects and the training in fixed routines of language production. Wittgenstein appears to endorse this view:[7] 'A child uses ... primitive forms of language ... when it learns to talk'. Here the teaching of language is not explanation, but training. And also,[8] 'the child, I should like to say, learns to react in such and such a way; and in so reacting it doesn't so far know anything. Knowing only begins at a later level'. The model that is suggested in these remarks is one in which early training in simple language games, in which words are used in routine ways, lays the foundation for later conceptually informed learning in which the learner exploits their capacity to think and reason about what they are doing.

For early word learning to be a case of learning by training it would need to be the case that human infants are trained by associating words with types of objects and that their early language use is restricted to following fixed routines. Anything more ambitious would have to wait upon the development of conceptual capacities to inform learning by reasoning. The empirical evidence shows that this developmental trajectory from learning by training to learning by reasoning is not borne out. The only model that fits the evidence is the model that sees basic word learning as learning by reasoning. The data only make sense on the basis of a rationalist model in which words are learnt by formulating and testing hypotheses. Young children need a rich repertoire of cognitive skills in order to engage in basic word learning. They do not acquire that repertoire by first being trained in fixed routines with words. In the beginning was the thought, not the word.

The basic evidence for the rationalist model of word learning can be summarised as follows. First, training is not required for children to learn a language. There are cultures in which adults do not speak to children until they are using some words meaningfully. Also, children who cannot speak but who can hear can nevertheless learn to understand complex syntactic structures and acquire a normal vocabulary. If someone cannot talk, they cannot get feedback on their speech. The basic mechanism for training, correction and reward by the parents, cannot be necessary for either vocabulary development or grasp of syntax.[9]

Second, if learning by training were the model for word learning, one would expect basic training to comprise experience of word/object association. This would be the primary experience to be rewarded and reinforced. But very young infants can cope with discrepant labelling. Discrepant labelling is when an adult names something that the infant has just been attending to after the infant has already switched her attention to something else.[10] Furthermore, even in supportive family environments, about 30–50% of the times that a word is used, young children are not attending to the object that the adult is talking about. For example, when the child hears 'Want a cookie?' they will be staring at someone's face. But 'cookie' doesn't mean face, and no child has thought that it does.[11]

Third, the vocabularies of young infants can be surprisingly abstract; they are not necessarily comprised of words for concrete things or, for that matter, observable things or events. Notwithstanding their impoverished perceptual experience, blind children learn words and often do so at the same rate as sighted children.[12]

Children cannot learn words by training, for the basic routines and associations are absent most of the time. Nevertheless, children learn words and do so at an astonishing rate. For Bloom, the only explanation for this that squares with the data is to recognise that 'children's learning of words requires rich mental capacities—conceptual, social, and linguistic—that interact in complicated ways'.[13] In learning their first words, the human infant is engaged in complicated mental activity. It is not just being trained in word/object associations, nor is it being trained by routines of language production coupled with routine experiences. The young infant is actively working out what is going on, what the adult speaker is trying to convey, where it should be looking to see what the adult is interested in, how best to interpret the adult's use of a word for something not present, etc. These are complex theoretical issues for the infant mind to grapple with. Human infants have to work out what to do with all this noise the adult is producing. They are not being trained. They learn by reasoning, by working out what is going on with all this noise.

The empirical evidence strongly supports the case for saying that some of the most basic learning that the human infant undertakes, the learning that first equips her with a stake in our shared culture, is learning by reasoning, not learning by training. If that empirical data is correct, we do well to consider very seriously just how robust the distinction between learning by training and learning by reasoning is. If we cannot appeal to it even at this most basic level of learning, we should be very cautious in assuming that it has any but the most superficial application in considering formal education later in life. What I want to do is to explore some of the philosophical issues surrounding the idea of learning by reasoning. I want to suggest that, in line with the empirical data regarding first language learning, there is no such thing as learning by training. I shall remain with considerations concerning language learning by providing a reading of Wittgenstein's account of the learning of words. At the most basic level of language acquisition, Wittgenstein appears to endorse the idea of learning by training. Nevertheless, even with quite simple language it makes best sense to read him as endorsing an account of learning by reasoning. Furthermore, getting clear what that means in Wittgenstein's treatment of language learning is instructive for understanding the idea of learning by reasoning in general.

3.

I want to suggest a way of reading two key examples about language learning in Wittgenstein's *Philosophical Investigations*. The examples are the discussion of family resemblances and the learning of the word 'game' from §65 and the passages from §145 onwards in which a pupil is being taught the meaning of 'add 2'. Both examples have been read as presenting a sceptical challenge regarding the learning of the meaning of words, although with the latter case, the rule-following argument is now more usually interpreted as generating a reductio argument rather than a sceptical argument. There is not consensus on the culprit assumption that is the target of the reductio. I want to suggest that both passages can be read as offering reductios of the idea of learning by training. The reductio is escaped by coming to appreciate the full richness of what constitutes learning by reasoning.

The suggestion that Wittgenstein endorses a model of learning by reasoning for language acquisition is at odds with the standard view of Wittgenstein. The standard view goes something like this. Wittgenstein's rule-following arguments show that language learning is radically underdetermined. However much the teacher says to the pupil in instructing them about the meaning of the word, it is compatible with an infinite number of possible meanings. When the pupil is invited to continue the use of the word, e.g. in continuing the arithmetical series generated by the phrase 'add 2', the teacher's explicit instruction leaves the pupil wholly unconstrained in what they do next. Grasp of meaning cannot be unconstrained, therefore teaching in language cannot be provided by explicit instruction. Rather than face the sceptical conclusion that there is no learning in meaning going on in this transaction, Wittgenstein is often taken as endorsing the thought that the learning transaction must be reconceived. Rather than see the transaction as one of explicit instruction, it is seen as training, training in a shared practice, a common form of behaviour. The pupil gets to understand the operation 'add 2' by being initiated or trained into a shared form of life. The idea here is that training is required to close down an otherwise crippling slack in the teaching transaction between what the teacher says and what needs to be learnt by the pupil. It seems that there is a profound gap between what is made explicit in the teacher's instruction and what has to be conveyed. Closing down that gap cannot be achieved by reasoning, hypothesis testing and the like, for that presupposes a common grasp of meaning is already in place and therefore begs the question.

Similarly, the moral standardly drawn from the discussion of the concept game in the earlier sections is a model that undermines the idea that concept learning is achieved by explicit instruction. Given the lack of necessary and sufficient conditions for the concept game, there can be no explicit instruction in the meaning of the word. The pupil being taught the word cannot be taught by explicit instruction in its meaning. They must learn to use the word in the rich filigree of connecting cases that make up the family resemblance of usage. And the standard way of understanding that idea is, again, to see the learning as an initiation into a practice of word use that cannot be articulated and rendered explicit. The learning is a form of training in this practice, a coming to use the word in the way that the language community does.

You might think that I am simplifying the distinction between learning by training and learning by reasoning, indeed, that I am producing a caricature of the former. Surely, you might protest, the notion of learning by training must be understood more generously than I have allowed. It comprises a training in 'practice' where this is understood in a generous way to allow that practices are normatively configured patterns of behaviour that have intrinsic standards of correctness and incorrectness. Training in practice is, in part, learning by reasoning for it involves acquiring a grasp of these intrinsic standards of correctness and incorrectness. I think this response is a fudge. It is a fudge that offers to endorse the common sense point of view that learning occurs when knowledgeable people tell less knowledgeable people things and the latter 'catch on' and pick up a complex normatively configured practice. The issue does not concern whether this common sense view is right, but our entitlement to endorse it. What I am calling the fudge gives no account of our entitlement to endorse this common sense picture. Nothing is gained by complicating the concept of training to include training in a practice, as the current objection conceives of it, without some account of how such training enables the learner to close down the slack—the gap between what is said by the teacher and what the pupil learns. The key issue here is: what is the activity that constitutes a practice and what kind of activity is it that is capable of closing down the slack between what the teacher says and what the pupil learns? Without a clear answer to these questions, we must enforce a sharp distinction between training and reasoning.

The options here are stark. The slack between what is said and what is learnt cannot, by hypothesis, be closed down by reasoning, by the learner working out for herself the meaning of the word. One way or another, any attempt by the pupil to work out for herself the meaning of the word would be a form of hypothesis testing. It would involve a substantive cognitive achievement. But if it is accepted that there is a gap between what is said and what is learnt, meaning is radically underdetermined and cannot be determined by such a cognitive achievement without begging the question. The pupil would already need to know about numbers, adding, the features of games, and so on, for her to be able to work out for herself the meaning of the word or phrase that the teacher is introducing. The problematic that Wittgenstein endorses on this standard reading is one in which the strategy of working out what the word means is simply unavailable to the pupil. It is a problematic that depends essentially on the idea of the gap between what is said and what is learnt and the consequent need to provide a means by which, despite that gap, the knowledge constitutive of understanding can be recovered. That is why it is a fudge to mess with the concept of training and include the idea of training in a practice. All that move does is posit a level of activity, practice, that has the capacity to close down the gap between what the teacher says and what the pupil learns, and it does this without giving any clear theoretical purchase on what is special about the activity of practice that enables it to achieve this. The fudge is basically a descriptive strategy that says, 'We get by'. That is not good enough. Nothing has been added to the notion of training to substantiate the idea of intrinsic normative standards. Until that is provided, we should read 'training' as an activity aimed at conformity in action, something instilled by mimesis.

Both examples are, then, properly interpreted on the standard reading as endorsing a model of learning as training; furthermore, a training that involves an initiation or acculturation into a shared activity. The fundamental aim of training is to take part in an activity by mimesis—conform first, think later, is the model. About the only thing right in the standard view is the negative thesis that the teaching of word meaning cannot be achieved by explicit instruction. Otherwise, what I am here calling the standard view gets Wittgenstein hopelessly wrong. It also misses central insights that he makes about the nature of learning.

What I am calling the standard view depends on the contrast between learning as explicitly codified instruction and training in a practice. This is one way of thinking about the contrast between learning by reasoning and learning by training. Coming to see what is wrong in the standard reading of Wittgenstein helps us to see that there is no adequate basis for thinking that the distinction between these different modes of learning is well made. This is not a clear-cut dichotomy. But it is not the concept of learning by training that needs rethinking as per the fudge; it is the concept of learning by reasoning—learning by the pupil working out for herself what to think and do. That is the interesting concept. The first thing that needs to be clarified is the idea of explicitly codified instruction.

The negative thesis is endorsed by Wittgenstein. In both cases—'game' and 'add 2'— the meaning of the word or phrase cannot be taught by providing an explicit articulation. Both cases indicate a restriction on the scope for making an explicit and fully codified articulation of meaning. In the case of 'game' the reason for this concerns the lack of a set of necessary and sufficient conditions that all games have in common. In the case of 'add 2', the reason concerns the more fundamental underdetermination of meaning that applies to any attempt to articulate meaning in an explicit statement. The latter case is more general, for even if there were an articulation available of the necessary and sufficient conditions that cases of adding 2 had in common, providing that articulation would not amount to rendering the meaning fully explicit. Any such account would require grasp of the meaning of the words used in that articulation. The explicit articulation of meaning is, then, always deferred. It presupposes a meaning that is not explicit.

There is a naïve response to this problematic that goes like this: If no attempt to render meaning explicit can work, why not accept the apparently fragmentary gestural explanations of meaning at face value as perfectly adequate explanations? Why try to render meaning explicit and then, when that fails, accept the training account as a way of closing the gap that the explicit account cannot address? In other words, why think that what we say when we explain meaning falls short of an explanation? This last question indicates Wittgenstein's fundamental insight about learning. I return to it in the next section.

Suppose the negative thesis that meaning cannot be rendered fully explicit is right. It does not follow from this that teaching someone the meaning of a word has to involve learning by training. The contrast with learning via explicitly codified instruction is not learning by training, where the latter is conceived as a habituation into shared routines—something that does not require the mental activity of working out what to think on behalf of the learner. If learning cannot be provided by explicitly codified instruction, it follows that the transaction between teacher and pupil cannot be conceived as a transaction in which the teacher provides an explicit and complete statement of the content of the learning to be acquired and the pupil receives that content. But that is no more than one extreme model of what learning by reasoning might amount to. The alternative to that does not have to be a model of learning by training.

The negative thesis amounts to no more than a non-codifiability claim about word meaning.[14] Knowledge of meaning cannot be codified into a body of theoretical knowledge, for any attempt to do so would have to presuppose knowledge of those words used to codify the knowledge. The transaction between teacher and pupil cannot, therefore, be modelled in terms of the transmission of a codified account of the word's meaning. What the pupil learns cannot be represented as a package of theoretical knowledge. It is not clear that this, in itself, is a significant result.

Grasp of the meaning of a word cannot be represented as theoretical knowledge. It must be represented therefore as a form of practical knowledge. Now, if learning by training means no more than learning by acquiring practical knowledge, it will then follow from Wittgenstein's negative thesis that learning the meaning of a word is a case of learning by training. But nothing illuminating has been said by this claim, for, thus far, this is not a concept of learning by training that contrasts with learning by reasoning. The critical issue is whether accepting the negative thesis that knowledge of meaning is not theoretical knowledge entails that there is a gap between what the teacher says and what the pupil has to come to know.

There is no reason to suppose that because a form of learning is not representable in terms of the acquisition of a body of theoretical knowledge, it must thereby be treated as a training that does not centrally involve the operation of reasoning, the mental activity of working out what to think. Of course, if you thought that doing something for a reason was always a matter of doing something that could be represented as acting on the basis of explicitly codified reasons that could be set out as an inference, matters might be different. With such a restrictive sense of doing something for a reason, the absence of an explicit theoretical representation of what you learn when you learn the meaning of 'add 2' would entail that you could not, in the restricted sense at issue, go on and act for a reason as you use the phrase in manifesting your understanding. Similarly, if what you know when you know the meaning of 'game' is not representable as a body of theoretical knowledge, then there is no explicit body of information that could form the basis of an explicit inference to provide a reason for your applying the word to a new case. But all that this shows is that it is a bad idea to work with such a limited conception of what it is to do something for a reason.

In contrast, if doing something for a reason is, however else one might characterise it, at least a matter of doing something so as to render oneself intelligible, then it is a doing something that must require some sensitivity to rational control and evaluation.[15] It will be a doing of things, including the use of language, which is directed and purposeful. Such a doing of things requires a repertoire of cognitive capacities for making sense of activities, capacities for directing activities so that they make sense. Directing activities is not a matter of having a fully codified script in advance of the doing from which the doing is directed. It need not, therefore, require a representation of the directedness that has to be first articulated and formulated in an explicitly codified way in order that it might then direct behaviour.[16] The point ought to be obvious, but it is typically missed. Getting this point right lies at the root of avoiding the charge of a simple innativism regarding capacities for reasoning.

Bloom's rationalist account of infant language learning runs counter to much received wisdom because it seems to require an extensive innatism. If language learning does not start with training—the development of routine associations between word and object/event, then the infant must already have rich cognitive capacities for making sense of the world and others prior to the acquisition of language. But that means that they must have the capacity to direct their behaviour prior to acquiring the language with which they label such organisation and direction. That is the point that leads Wittgenstein to charge that Augustine's model of language learning is, in effect, a model of second language learning, for it requires that the infant already has a language. How else, otherwise, would they be able to direct their behaviour prior to learning the adult's language? The question is misplaced, for the assumption on which it depends is false. The assumption is that in order to direct one's behaviour with respect to some object or feature, one must have a language that codes for that object or feature. But that assumption simply begs the question in favour of a simple empiricism about learning, the empiricism that sees learning by training as the basic form of learning. What Augustine's model requires is a more modest assumption: that the infant has a capacity to direct its behaviour with respect to X independently of having a language that codes for X. And that is not an unreasonable assumption to make.[17] If we attend carefully to Wittgenstein's own words, we find Wittgenstein agrees.

4.

The negative thesis is the thesis that the meaning of a word cannot be fully codified and rendered in an explicit instruction. If that is right, then we cannot treat knowledge of meaning as akin to theoretical knowledge. I assume that Wittgenstein endorses the negative thesis. It is commonplace to hold that it follows from the negative thesis that our explanations of meaning fail to determine meaning, that what we are able to say to the pupil leaves the meaning of the word underdetermined. That is the standard view that the negative thesis entails a slack between what is said by the teacher and what needs to be grasped by the pupil. The response then is either to accept the scepticism about meaning that the existence of this gap reveals, or to try to close the gap by invoking training into shared forms of activity. As already noted, if the situation is set up in this way, the activity that closes the gap must be an activity into which, in the first instance, the pupil is trained. The activity cannot be the mental activity of working out what the teacher means, for that would be to ascribe to the pupil a complex of cognitive capacities that endow them with something as complex as the meaning they are supposedly being taught. If you accept both the negative thesis and the idea of the gap between what is said and what is learnt, then the only legitimate way of closing that gap is by introducing the concept of learning by training. Anything richer than that at that point is a fudge.

The above is not, however, Wittgenstein's position. Wittgenstein has a central role for activity and practical knowledge in giving an account of word learning, but the place for activity is not that identified in the previous paragraph. Indeed, the site of activity that Wittgenstein permits is the same as that suggested in Bloom's account of infant language learning. In the standard reading of Wittgenstein, the role of training is to fill the gap between what the teacher says and the pupil learns. But recall the naïve response I noted in the previous section. The naïve response allows that although the transaction between teacher and pupil is not the conveyance of theoretical knowledge, there is no gap between what the teacher says and what the pupil learns. Why think that what we say when we explain meaning falls short of an explanation? Consider Wittgenstein's own words:

> How should we explain to someone what a game is? I imagine that we should describe *games* to him, and we might add: 'This *and similar things* are called "games"'. And do we know any more about it ourselves? Is it only other people whom we cannot tell exactly what a game is?—But this is not ignorance. (Wittgenstein, 1953, §69)

The idea that there is a gap between what the teacher says and the pupil must learn is the idea that what the teacher says short-changes the pupil; it falls short of what they must pick up. The teacher is left unable to articulate explicitly what they intend the pupil to learn. This would seem to introduce a form of ignorance into the scene. The teacher has failed to say quite what they know. But Wittgenstein explicitly denies that this is ignorance. When we say things like 'this and similar things are called "games"' we say *exactly* what we know. This is what we know and it is not a form of ignorance.

Further, if there is a gap between what is said and what is learnt, then given that our attempts at teaching are doomed to fall short of a full explicit statement of our knowledge, what we say must be conceived as indirect evidence for what the pupil has to pick up. But Wittgenstein denies this too:

> [T]his is just how one might explain to someone what a game is. One gives examples and intends them to be taken in a particular way.—I do not, however, mean by this that he is supposed to see in those examples that common thing which I—for some reason—was unable to express; but that he is now to *employ* those examples in a particular way. Here giving examples is not an *indirect* means of explaining—in default of a better. (Wittgenstein, 1953, §71)

This section is especially important, for it shows that 'taking the examples in a particular way' is not a matter of catching on where the pupil extends the fragmentary information offered by the teacher into a correct and full account of understanding; what it means to take the examples aright concerns what the pupil *does*. It is what the pupil goes on to do that matters, not what information they generate on the basis of the indirect prompts supplied by the teacher.

I think the best way of understanding these remarks is to see them as endorsing a rationalist model of learning, not unlike Bloom's account of early language learning. It is a model that turns our normal way of thinking about learning on its head. Suppose knowing the meaning of a word is neither knowing something (theory) nor knowing how to act (behaviour/training) but knowing how to work out how to render speakers intelligible. It is a matter of knowing how to engage in a project of reasoning and enquiry. This is compatible with the negative thesis that understanding meaning is not possessing theoretical knowledge. But it does not follow from the negative thesis that our explanations of meaning fail to determine meaning. The aim in teaching meaning is neither to convey information (theory) nor to convey behaviour (training); it is to get the pupil to *join in* an activity of making themselves and others intelligible. It is to get the pupil to join in the activity of reasoning. And the activity involved here is not the overt public activity of taking part in a common habit; it is the mental activity of making sense of things. What we say when explaining the meaning of words is, as Wittgenstein allows, precisely enough *if we assume that the pupil is a subject with a capacity for reasoning, a capacity for directing and organising their behaviour to make sense of themselves and others.* If we assume that, then we say plenty when we say, 'This and similar things are called "games"'. There is no more a puzzle about the gap between what the teacher says and the pupil learns than there is a gap between what talkative adults say and do and what human infants learn from this. In both cases, what the pupil learns is to join in an activity of reasoning and, by so doing, to extend that activity.[18]

Wittgenstein endorses the negative thesis but not the idea of the gap between what is said and what is understood. Without that gap, there is no need for training. There is a need for activity, for agency. But the place of that activity is not to fill a gap by taking part in public behaviour. It is to engage the mental activity of reasoning. The only gap is in our own impoverished understanding of what learning is and might be.

The account of learning that I have just sketched is one that requires a rethinking of the activity central to learning. But it is not a rethinking that adds to the description of public practices. It is a rethinking of activity that requires, in turn, a rethinking of the subject, the agent whose most basic activity is the mental activity of reasoning. Acknowledging the centrality of that activity in learning redraws the boundaries of empowerment too. Acknowledging the pupil as essentially an active reasoner is to empower them. This is not the kind of empowerment that comes from granting them a body of knowledge that gives them power. It is not the empowerment that comes from recognition by the group. It is the empowerment that comes from acknowledging that the pupil is an active reasoner, a judge, not a mimic, someone who in response to the teacher's invitation to join in the business of reasoning and making sense of ourselves, does so with autonomy and, oftentimes, alacrity.[19]

Notes

1. For more on the concept of judgement, see Luntley, 2005.
2. The claim that such learning requires reasoning should not be taken to require explicit formal argumentation. The notion of reasoning might be interpreted in a number of ways. At its most liberal, 'reasoning' need require no more than a mental activity by which the subject makes a transition in their view of what to think and what to do that renders their behaviour intelligible. It is then a separate and contentious thesis that only transitions capable of being modelled as explicit inferences count as transitions that render a subject's behaviour intelligible. See Luntley, 2005 for more on this.
3. In Luntley, 2003 I emphasised what I am now calling the rationalist element in Wittgenstein's treatment of word learning and suggested that the discussion of training could be read in a way that made it party to a rationalist approach. That reading was, perhaps, a little too generous to Wittgenstein. For further discussion of this and of some of the interpretational issues involved see Luntley, 2007.
4. Here is Dummett for one endorsing the distinction and the primacy of learning by training:

   A child at this stage has no linguistic knowledge but merely a training in certain linguistic practices. When he has reached a stage at which it is possible for him to lie, his utterances will have ceased to be merely responses to features of the environment or to experienced needs. They will have become purposive actions based upon a knowledge of their significance to others. (Dummett, 1991, p. 95)

5. Bloom, 2001, p. 1103.
6. Bloom, 2000.
7. Wittgenstein, 1953, §5.
8. Wittgenstein, 1974, §538.
9. Bloom, 2000, p. 8.

10. Cf. Baldwin, 1995.
11. Bloom, 2000, p. 58.
12. Op cit., p. 59.
13. Op cit., p. 1.
14. The negative thesis is the denial of the following model. Suppose grasp of meaning is representable in terms of a capacity to manipulate elements within a symbolic system like, for example, a formal language. Understanding the meaning of a word would then be modelled in terms of knowing the word's role within that symbolic system. If you think of the system as like a formal language, it can then seem reasonable to suppose that any given word has a fixed role within the language and that role can be articulated and stated as a fact about the system. Now, if the negative thesis is right, this model cannot be right. That means that learning the meaning of a word cannot be modelled in terms of something akin to learning one's way around the structure of a formal system. But all that amounts to is the non-codifiability of a word's meaning.
15. It is what McDowell would call acting within the space of reasons.
16. My research on expertise is concerned with cataloguing and accounting for the situated reasoning of experienced professionals, such as classroom teachers, who organise and direct their behaviour without a codified account of what they are doing. They act without a script for their directedness by deploying attentional skills that enable them to 'lock-on' and adapt their behaviour to the particular contingencies of the environment with which they deal. This is reasoning—the rational enterprise of making oneself intelligible. See the report on the AHRB funded pilot project, 'Attention and the knowledge bases of expertises' at http://www2.warwick.ac.uk/fac/soc/philosophy/research/akbep. The project on expertise is part of a larger enterprise of understanding the first-person perspective of reasoning—the wilful directed working out of what to do and what to think and say that we all practice. If we ask the question: What are the ingredients of this activity, the capacities by which we achieve this working out of what to do and think? then to say, lamely, that it is part of a practice, is to fail to engage in a substantive philosophical enterprise of the study of reasoning and the capacities on which it draws.
17. There is much more to be said on this. One issue concerns whether Augustine over intellectualises the infant mind. That might be the case, but does not detract from the key Augustinian insight that the infant mind has a will, a capacity for directedness of its attention and behaviour. Getting Augustine right is also a matter of getting Wittgenstein right on quite what he means by 'natural history'. Is this just a body of dispositions, something provided by training? Or does it include the capacity for directedness? If the latter, then not so much differentiates Wittgenstein from Augustine. For more on this, see Luntley, 2007.
18. The notion of joining in does not require a constructivist construal of learning and of the meaning of words. Learning by joining in is, of course, a social activity, but the activity that the pupil joins in with is not intrinsically social; it is the activity of reasoning. On my model, that is something individualistic, for it is based in the pupil's capacity to direct action. That is the individualistic basis of reasoning. Learning by reasoning takes place both individualistically and socially when two or more people are involved, e.g. teacher and pupil. But that does not entail social constructivism; it entails the platitude that social action involves two or more people coordinating their behaviour.
19. I am indebted to my colleague Stephen Butterfill for advice on the psychological literature on early language learning. A first draft of this paper was presented at the Institute of Education, London in autumn 2005 before presentation at the 34th Annual PESA Conference, *Critical Thinking and Learning: Values, concepts and issues*, Hong Kong, November 2005. Thanks to all present on those occasions, but colleagues in London and Hong Kong will understand if I take this (last) opportunity to single out the late Terry McLaughlin whose gentle but perceptive comments at the London session helped so much, as ever, in bringing things into focus. Thanks Terry.

References

Baldwin, D. (1995) Understanding the Link Between Joint Attention and Language, in: C. Moore & D Frye (eds), *Joint Attention: Its origins and role in development* (Hove, Erlbaum).
Bloom, P. (2000) *How Children Learn the Meaning of Words* (Cambridge, MA, MIT Press).
Bloom, P. (2001) Précis of How Children Learn the Meaning of Words, *Behavioral and Brain Sciences*, 24:6, pp. 1095–1103.
Dummett, M. (1991) *The Logical Basis of Metaphysics* (London, Duckworth).
Luntley, M. (2003) *Wittgenstein: Meaning and judgement* (Oxford & New York, Blackwell).
Luntley, M. (2005) The Role of Judgement, *Philosophical Explorations*, Special Issue, Competences: Educational Philosophy of Minded Agency, edited by J. Bransen & M. Luntley, pp. 279–93.
Luntley, M. (2007) The Teaching and Learning of Words, in: D. Levy & E. Zamuner (eds), *Wittgenstein's Enduring Arguments* (New York & London, Routledge, forthcoming).
Wittgenstein, L. (1953) *Philosophical Investigations*, trans. G. E. M. Anscombe (Oxford, Blackwell).
Wittgenstein, L. (1974) *On Certainty*, trans. & ed. G. E. M. Anscombe & G. H. von Wright (Oxford, Blackwell).

7

Is Popper's Falsificationist Heuristic a Helpful Resource for Developing Critical Thinking?

CHI-MING LAM
The University of Hong Kong

Three Core Concepts of Critical Rationalism

Formulated fundamentally by Popper as an attitude of admitting that '*I may be wrong and you may be right, and by an effort, we may get nearer to the truth*' (1966, p. 225), critical rationalism is an attitude of readiness to listen to critical arguments and to learn from our mistakes. Near the end of his life, Popper revealed that he owes the idea of this formulation to what a young Carinthian member of the National Socialist Party, not long before the year in which Hitler came to power in Germany (1933), said to him: 'What, you want to argue? I don't argue: I shoot!' (1996, p. xiii). The young man's readiness to shoot rather than to argue may indeed have planted the seeds of three core concepts of Popper's critical rationalism, viz. fallibilism ('I may be wrong'), criticism (the required 'effort'), and verisimilitude ('we may get nearer to the truth').

By fallibilism Popper (1966) intends the view that we are fallible and that the quest for certainty is mistaken. While the former view can be substantiated historically by the fact that what we once thought to be well-established may later turn out to be false, the latter can be understood theoretically by the problem that what we can explain or know is limited. One such limitation concerns the power of our brain to explain: according to Hayek (1952), any apparatus of classification must possess a structure of a higher degree of complexity than that possessed by the objects which it classifies; it implies that no explaining agent can ever explain objects of its own kind or own degree of complexity, and thus that the human brain can never fully explain its own operations. Another limitation arises from our inability to predict the future course of history, not least because of our inability to predict the future growth of human knowledge: as Popper puts it, 'if there is such a thing as growing human knowledge, then we cannot anticipate today what we shall know only tomorrow' (2002a, p. xii). Accordingly, his fallibilism denies the possibility of certain knowledge and of authoritative sources of knowledge. Instead, he asserts that nothing is secure and that our knowledge remains conjectural and fallible.

However, because we can learn from our mistakes, fallibilism need not cause any sceptical or relativist conclusions. And criticism, he claims, 'is the only way we have of detecting our mistakes, and of learning from them in a systematic way' (1966, p. 376). It includes criticizing the theories or conjectures not only of others but also of our own. Since, for Popper (1989), criticism invariably consists in pointing out some contradiction (within the theory criticized, or between the theory and another theory which we have some reason to accept, or between the theory and certain statements of facts), deductive logical reasoning is suggested as *the* method of criticism: only by purely deductive reasoning can we discover what our theories imply, and thus where contradictions lie. More specifically, the importance of deductive or formal logic to criticism lies in the fact that it adopts the rules by which truth is transmitted from premises to conclusions while falsity is re-transmitted from conclusions to premises. It is this re-transmission of falsity that 'makes formal logic the *Organon of rational criticism*—that is, of refutation' (ibid., p. 64). In fact, rejecting all attempts at the justification of theories, Popper replaces justi- fication with criticism in his non-justificationist or falsificationist view of rational- ity: 'Previously, most philosophers had thought that any claim to rationality meant rational *justification* (of one's beliefs); my thesis was, at least since my *Open Society*, that rationality meant rational *criticism* (of one's own theory and of competing theories)' (2002b, p. 173). However, considering a theory may stand up to criticism better than its competitors, he concedes that we can sometimes 'justify' our *preference* for a theory in the *negative* sense that a theory receives some kind of support if it has, rather than secured positive evidence, withstood severe criticism.

The idea of getting nearer to the truth or achieving greater verisimilitude is crucial to Popper's concept of critical rationalism, for it is only the idea of truth that allows us to speak sensibly of fallibilism and criticism: the purpose of searching for mistakes and eliminating as many of them as we possibly can through critical discussion is to get nearer to the truth. Criticizing subjective theories of truth for conceiving truth as something we are justified in believing or in accepting in accordance with some criterion of well-foundedness, Popper (1989) adopts Tarski's correspondence theory of objective truth that a statement is true if and only if it corresponds to the facts. For one thing, Tarski's objective theory of truth allows us to make certain assertions that appear obviously correct to Popper but self- contradictory within those subjective theories of truth: for example, a theory may be true even if nobody believes it, and even if we have no reason to think it true; another theory may be false even if we have comparatively good reasons for accepting it; we search for truth, but may not know when we have found it; and we have no criterion of truth, but are guided by the idea of truth as a regulative principle. To allay suspicions about the idea of getting nearer to the truth, or of the growth of knowledge, Popper (1979) introduces a logical idea of verisimilitude by combining two notions from Tarski, viz. truth and content. Defining the class of all true statements and false statements following from a statement p as the truth content and falsity content of p respectively, Popper explains that:

Intuitively speaking, a theory T_1 has less verisimilitude than a theory T_2 if and only if (a) their truth contents and falsity contents (or their measures) are comparable, and either (b) the truth content, but not the falsity content, of T_1 is smaller than that of T_2, or else (c) the truth content of T_1 is not greater than that of T_2, but its falsity content is greater. (Ibid., p. 52)

He accordingly regards the search for verisimilitude rather than truth as a more realistic aim of science in that while we can never have sufficiently good arguments for claiming that we have actually attained the truth, we can have reasonably good arguments for claiming that we may have made progress towards the truth (i.e. that the theory T_2 is nearer to the truth and thus preferable to its predecessor T_1).

Stratagems Opposed to Criticism

Yet, to put such a falsificationist theory into practice, it is necessary to identify and combat a nest of philosophical presuppositions that work against criticism and help to confine individuals to the justificationist framework. As the Chinese proverb cautions, 'It is easy to dodge an open spear thrust but difficult to guard against an arrow shot from behind', one is unlikely to circumvent or eliminate the effects of these anti-criticism presuppositions unless various hidden stratagems that reduce and eschew criticism are themselves exposed to criticism. Popper, as an advocate of falsificationism, spares no pains to reveal such protective or evasive stratagems. To begin with, he (1989) points out that the doctrine that truth is manifest runs counter to the doctrine of fallibility and thus of tolerance: if truth were manifest, we would be unlikely to make mistakes, and thus would not need to tolerate or pardon others for their mistakes committed as a result of their prejudices. Since criticism involves searching for errors of our own and of others, which assumes that we are prone to errors and consequently should be tolerant of others, the doctrine that truth is manifest is diametrically opposed to it. Another stratagem Popper combats is the demand for precision in concepts as a prerequisite for criticism or problem-solving. Affirming the non-existence of 'precise' concepts, or concepts with 'sharp boundary lines', Popper (ibid.) emphasizes that words are significant only as tools for formulating theories and don't need to be more precise than our problems demand. To deal with the problem that our problems may sometimes demand that we make new distinctions for the sake of clarity or precision, he suggests an *ad hoc* approach:

> If because of lack of clarity a misunderstanding arises, do not try to lay new and more solid foundations on which to build a more precise 'conceptual framework', but reformulate your formulations *ad hoc*, with a view to avoiding those misunderstandings which have arisen or which you can foresee. And always remember that *it is impossible to speak in such a way that you cannot be misunderstood*: there will always be some who misunderstand you. (Popper, 2002b, p. 29)

Popper identifies further three approaches that work against criticism, namely essentialism, instrumentalism, and conventionalism. Essentialism assumes that science aims at ultimate explanations that describe the 'essences' of things—the realities that lie behind appearances—and therefore are neither in need nor susceptible of further explanation. Popper (1989) criticizes essentialism as obscurantist in the sense that it prevents fruitful questions or further criticisms from being raised. He (ibid.) also condemns as obscurantist the instrumentalist view of theories as mere instruments for prediction, because it stresses application but neglects falsification or criticism: for instrumental purposes of practical application, a theory may continue to be used within the limits of its applicability even after its refutation—in other words, a theory cannot be falsified insofar as it is interpreted as a simple instrument, for it can always be said that different theories have different ranges of application. And with respect to conventionalist philosophy, which regards laws of nature as our own creations and arbitrary conventions rather than representations of nature, although Popper admits that it deserves credit for clarifying the relations between theory and experiment, or rather for recognizing 'the importance ... of the part played by our actions and operations, planned in accordance with conventions and deductive reasoning, in conducting and interpreting our scientific experiments' (1980, p. 80), he rejects its methods of protecting the theoretical systems of the natural sciences against criticism. He asserts that there are at least four conventionalist stratagems—introducing *ad hoc* hypotheses, modifying ostensive definitions, adopting a sceptical attitude to the reliability of the experimenter, and casting doubt on the acumen of the theoretician—which make it impossible to falsify these systems.

A Bias Towards Confirmation

The Pervasiveness and Various Guises of the Confirmation Bias

Apart from exposing to criticism the various hidden stratagems that work against it, it is also important to combat what appears a common psychological tendency of humans to be biased towards confirmation, or against disconfirmation, a tendency that reflects a conflict between falsificationism and apparently deep-rooted psychological mechanisms. Unfortunately, Popper did not give much attention to this. According to Nickerson (1998), confirmation bias connotes an unwitting process of seeking or interpreting evidence in ways that are partial to existing beliefs or hypotheses. A great deal of empirical evidence supports the view that the confirmation bias not only is extensive and strong but also appears in various guises: reflected in the tendency of people, for example, to demand less hypothesis-consistent evidence for accepting a hypothesis than hypothesis-inconsistent information for rejecting a hypothesis (Pyszczynski & Greenberg, 1987); to recall or produce reasons supporting the side they favour rather than the other side on a controversial issue (Baron, 1995); and, when assessing the validity of a conditional 'if p then q', to seek for the presence of p and q so as to confirm the conditional rather than for the presence of p and *not-q* so as to disconfirm the conditional (Wason, 1966).

Although Polya (1954) has argued that what distinguishes scientists from ordinary people is their disposition to seek disconfirmatory evidence for their hypotheses, instances of confirmation bias still abound in the history of science. This can be illustrated at two—personal and institutional—levels. At the personal level, Michael Faraday advocated ignoring disconfirmatory evidence when dealing with a novel hypothesis until the hypothesis was well-confirmed (Tweney, 1989), while Robert Millikan reported only those observations that fitted his hypothesis when publishing experimental work on determining the electric charge of a single electron (Henrion & Fischhoff, 1986). At the institutional level, just as Newton's concept of universal gravity was rejected by Huygens and Leibniz due to their resistance to the idea of a force not reducible to matter and motion extending throughout space, scientific discoveries have often met with resistance from scientists themselves, especially from those whose theoretical positions were challenged by the discoveries. The typical reaction of scientists to the challenge of anomalous data to an existing theory is in fact to challenge the data first and, if the data prove reliable, then to complicate the theory just enough to accommodate the anomalous result (Nickerson, 1998). Perhaps Polya's characterization of individual scientists as being inclined to disconfirm their own hypotheses is half correct at most: they appear eager to criticize or disconfirm other scientists' hypotheses rather than theirs.

Theoretical Explanations for the Confirmation Bias

With regard to the question of how to account for the confirmation bias, apart from what Matlin and Stang (1978) dub the Pollyanna principle, which explains in a commonsensical way that people tend to be partial towards pleasant thoughts and memories rather than unpleasant ones and thus to believe propositions they would like to be true rather than those they would prefer to be false, there are at least four theoretical explanations that various researchers have proposed. First, according to Nickerson, people are basically limited to consideration of only one thing— and inclined to gather information about only one hypothesis—at a time. However, restricting attention to a single hypothesis might strengthen that hypothesis even if it is false:

> An incorrect hypothesis can be sufficiently close to being correct that it receives a considerable amount of positive reinforcement, which may be taken as further evidence of the correctness of the hypothesis in hand and inhibit continued search for an alternative. (Nickerson, 1998, p. 198)

Hence the confirmation bias.

Second, discounting the possibility that people seek deliberately to confirm rather than disconfirm their hypotheses, Evans (1989) attributes the confirmation bias not to their motivation to confirm but to their failure to think in explicitly disconfirmatory terms. His argument accords with much evidence that people find it more difficult to deal with negative than positive information. For example, it is more difficult to decide the truth or falsity of negative sentences than of positive ones (Wason, 1961); and inferences from negative premises need more time to evaluate and are more likely to be evaluated wrongly than those from positive premises (Fodor, Fodor, & Garrett, 1975).

Third, just as Friedrich asserts that 'our inference processes are first and foremost pragmatic, survival mechanisms and only secondarily truth detection strategies' (1993, p. 298), the judgements people make in many real-life situations are motivated more by a desire to achieve success and survival—and thus to balance potential rewards against perceived risks—than by the objective of determining the truth or falsity of hypotheses. This explains why confirmation bias may result when the undesirable consequences of considering a true hypothesis as false are greater than those of considering a false hypothesis as true.

Last, stressing the importance of being able to justify what one believes at all levels of education can establish or strengthen a tendency to seek confirmatory evidence selectively: if one is always stimulated to adduce reasons for opinions that one holds and is not urged also to articulate reasons that could be given against them, one is being trained to exercise a confirmation bias (Nickerson, 1998). To make matters worse, some educational practices fail to distinguish explicitly between case-building (i.e. seeking selectively or giving undue weight to evidence that supports one's position while neglecting to seek or discounting evidence that would tell against it) and evidence-weighing (i.e. seeking evidence on all sides and evaluating it as objectively as one can) so that what is in reality case-building passes for the impartial evaluation of evidence: hence the ubiquity and strength of the confirmation bias among educated adults. A typical example of such case-building educational practices is debate, in which debaters give their primary attention to arguments that support the positions they are defending—even if they might advance potential counter-arguments, their intention is only to reveal the shortcomings of these counter-arguments. After all, debaters aim to win, and the way to do so is to make the strongest possible case for their own position while countering, discounting, or simply ignoring any evidence that might be brought against it.

The Teacher's Role in Undermining the Strength and Spread of the Confirmation Bias

Although it can be argued that the confirmation bias helps both to protect our sense of self by rendering our preferred beliefs less vulnerable than they otherwise would be (Greenwald, 1980) and to guard science against indiscriminate acceptance of alleged new discoveries that fail to stand the test of time (Price, 1963), the bias is still generally regarded as a human failing: it can contribute to the formation of various delusions, the development and survival of superstitions, and the perpetuation of hostility and strife between people with conflicting views of the world (Nickerson, 1998). It is probably a good idea to start with the education of children if the strength and spread of the confirmation bias are to be undermined and checked. What then are the implications for educational practice? First, teachers themselves should be aware of the confirmation bias—its pervasiveness and the various guises in which it appears. Such awareness could help students to be more cautious in making decisions about important issues and more open to opinions that differ from their own.

Considering, moreover, that the confirmation bias is partly attributed to the tendency of people to consider only one hypothesis at a time, teachers should encourage their students to think of several alternative hypotheses simultaneously in attempting to explain a phenomenon. The discovery by Tweney *et al.* that individuals seldom employ this thinking strategy successfully—for they prefer 'to evaluate several pieces of data against a single hypothesis, rather than one datum against several hypotheses' (1980, p. 119)—demonstrates the superiority of working in groups in learning to avoid the bias: having each individual work on a different hypothesis, groups can keep track of several hypotheses at the same time.

Teachers should also realize the significance of making explicit the distinction between case-building and evidence-weighing, and encourage their students to evaluate evidence objectively in the formation and evaluation of hypotheses. Here it is vital to cultivate in students a critical mindset that prompts them to think of reasons both for and (especially) against any judgement that is to be made. And they should be made aware that the motivation to find support for preferred beliefs 'often leads a person to overlook even glaring faults in the data, because it is difficult to find what is not sought' (Dawson, Gilovich, & Regan, 2002, p. 1386).

Despite the inclination of scientists to discount data inconsistent with their theory, Fugelsang *et al.* (2004) found that scientists began to modify their original theory when repeated observations of inconsistent data occurred. Indeed, the initial reluctance of scientists to accept inconsistent data and their subsequent re-theorization through repeated experimentation can be considered as a practical heuristic device: it prevents them from prematurely accepting findings that may be spurious while permitting the revision of theories and thus the growth of knowledge. In the realm of science teaching, this heuristic device should be introduced to students, particularly for fostering an appropriate attitude towards inconsistent data.

Can Students Be Taught to Falsify?

Influential as Popper is in the philosophy and practice of science, a question can still be raised about the effectiveness of his methodology, for there is much controversy in the psychological literature over the feasibility and utility of falsification as a strategy for solving scientific problems. To start with, many psychological studies show that many scientists have difficulty in disconfirmatory reasoning. For instance, in a survey conducted by Mahoney and Kimper (1976), a sample of physicists, biologists, sociologists and psychologists were asked to rate the validity of four forms of material implication (i.e. to judge whether it is valid, assuming that p materially implies q, to infer q from p, *not-q* from *not-p*, p from q, and *not-p* from *not-q*) and to identify the logically critical experiments that could test the validity of a hypothesis of the form 'if p then q'. It was found that over half of these scientists failed to recognize *modus tollens* (i.e. the inference from *not-q* to *not-p*) as logically valid, and that fewer than 10% of them were able to select correctly the experiments that had the critical potential of falsifying the sample hypothesis. Perhaps more surprisingly, similar difficulty in recognizing the logical validity of falsification was found in a sample of statisticians who had been formally trained in testing statistical (null) hypotheses and thus in examining possible disconfirming evidence (Einhorn & Hogarth, 1978).

However, having difficulty in using disconfirmatory reasoning does not mean a lack of ability to do so. Indeed, some researchers have successfully taught college students to employ disconfirmatory strategies to solve such reasoning problems as Wason's (1960) 2-4-6 problem and Gardner's (1977) 'New Eleusis'. Wason advanced the 2–4-6 problem as a test of inductive reasoning: subjects were told that the sequence of three numbers '2-4-6' was an instance of a rule that the experimenter had in mind (the rule was 'any three numbers in ascending order'); they were required to discover the rule by generating their own test sequences of three numbers which the experimenter would describe to them as correct or incorrect instances of the rule. Considering Wason's subjects displayed a strong confirmation bias and tended to generate test sequences consistent with their tentative hypotheses, Tweney *et al.* (1980), using the same 2–4-6 task, made an attempt to teach disconfirmatory strategies to their subjects, that is, to ask their subjects to try generating disconfirmatory instances. They found that the mean number of confirmatory and disconfirmatory instances generated by subjects in the disconfirmatory group was 1.5 and 6.6 respectively (in Experiment 1). This indicates that Tweney *et al.* were successful in eliminating most attempts at confirmation and thus in changing the inquiry strategy of those subjects in the disconfirmatory group.

'New Eleusis' is a card game designed to simulate the inductive search for truth. Gorman, Gorman, Latta, and Cunningham (1984) adapted it to create a task for studying scientific reasoning: subjects were asked to guess what the underlying rule behind a sequence of cards was by playing cards one at a time (one of the rules, for instance, was 'a difference of 1 must separate adjacent cards'); they would be informed by the experimenter whether their cards were right or wrong but would not receive any feedback from the experimenter on whether their guesses were right or wrong until the end of the experiment. Using this task to study how confirmatory, disconfirmatory, and combined strategies affected group problem solving (in Experiment 2), they instructed their subjects to concentrate respectively on getting as many cards right as possible, on getting as many cards wrong as possible, and on getting cards right until they had a guess which was then tested by playing cards that would be wrong. They found that disconfirmatory groups played incorrect cards 41% of the time, combined groups 33% of the time, and confirmatory groups only 20% of the time. Again, the result shows that the instructional manipulation was successful; hence the feasibility of inducing the use of disconfirmation.

Two Contributory Factors in Eliciting Disconfirmation

Here, two contributory factors in the higher use of disconfirmation—collaborative reasoning and lower normativity—need attention if disconfirmatory strategies are to be promoted in the classroom. To illustrate how group processes often facilitated disconfirmation, Gorman *et al.* (1984, p. 75) provided the following brief exchange between two subjects in one disconfirmatory group:

> One subject complained to the other group members: 'I have a hard time guessing wrong'. Another subject tried to tell her how to disconfirm: 'If you

think the series goes like this (pointing to a sequence of cards ascending by ones),
try to prove it wrong by putting down a card that doesn't go with the series'.

The second subject soon induced not only the first subject but also other group members to falsify more and more guesses. Such beneficial effects of peer inter-action are echoed in the study of Moshman and Geil (1998), who found that while 75% of the subjects in interactive groups could apply correctly a disconfirmatory strategy in testing a hypothesis, only 9% of the individual subjects working in isolation could do so. As close examination of the videotaped group discussions revealed little evidence of passive conformity to majority views or to the views of an apparent expert but a usual attempt to co-construct a consensus solution—a structure of arguments qualitatively more sophisticated than that generated by most individuals—by sharing perspectives and reasons, they attributed the superior per-formance of the groups to collaborative reasoning rather than to peer pressure or imitation. Insight into the logic of falsification appears to be more readily achieved in collaborative reasoning than in individual reasoning.

The question whether disconfirmation is used during collaborative hypothesis testing might, however, depend upon the type of relation reasoners have with their partners and with the experimenter: the study of Butera, Caverni and Rossi (2005) showed that while confrontation with a low-competence partner rendered subjects able to learn to use disconfirmation, confrontation with a high-competence partner induced them to use confirmation, even when the partner used disconfirmation. A possible explanation is that confrontation with a high-competence partner could threaten subjects' sense of competence, thereby leading them to test their own hypotheses through confirmation as a defensive strategy that seems to support their hypotheses and thus to protect their competence; in contrast, a low-competence partner is less likely to threaten the subjects' sense of competence, thereby allowing them the opportunity to test the limits of the validity of their own hypotheses through disconfirmation (ibid.). Moreover, Butera *et al.* (2005) showed that sub-jects who were confronted with the violation of a conversational rule—i.e. were told by the experimenter in solving Wason's (1960) 2–4-6 problem that 2–4-6 was *not* a good example of the rule and had been chosen only to show them what was a number triad—used a high proportion of disconfirmation, whatever the compe-tence of the partner. They explained that disconfirmation stemmed from the pos-sibility of diverging from not only social norms in the case of interaction and social influence (e.g. the constraining power of competence), but also conversational norms in the case of language (e.g. the constraining power of the example given by the experimenter): considering the high-status experimenter might lead subjects through conversation to focus on the given triad, to formulate a hypothesis that captured all the salient features of the triad, and to try to confirm it, telling them that 2–4-6 was not a good example of the rule might break the focused processing of the task and lead them to use disconfirmation. It appears therefore that people use confirmation in constraining reasoning situations but that 'the use of disconfir-mation can be increased by lowering the normativity of the situation, either by a less threatening source or by less constraining conversational rules' (ibid., p. 186).

In other words, if disconfirmation is to be taught effectively to students, merely creating the opportunity for them to collaborate with each other is not enough. The teacher should also attempt to lower the normativity of the learning environment by such means as ensuring that students interacting within the group are not threatening or dominating, and avoiding proposing as an authority a model solution to them during problem-solving. The latter is particularly noteworthy in that many teachers really see themselves as an authority in the classroom who, they think, should know the answer to every question. Such an authoritative image teachers have of their role is detrimental to the adoption of disconfirmation in two ways: first, it makes the interaction between the teacher and students more normative; and second, it makes the classroom less likely to satisfy the basic requirement for implementing falsificationism in education, that is, to become a place that values mistakes made by both teachers and students (Sankey, 1999).

The Influence of the Complexity of the Problem

Despite the foregoing evidence in support of the argument that people can be taught to falsify their hypotheses, some studies have shown that instructional manipulations might fail to elicit falsification when the inference problem turns complex. For example, to achieve a more realistic simulation of science in their study, Mynatt, Doherty and Tweney (1977) designed a rather complex inference task: after observing a set of computer displays made up of stationary geometric figures and moving particles whose motion was influenced by the figures, subjects were asked to discover the laws that governed the motion of particles by first generating a hypothesis and then choosing the appropriate experiments to test that hypothesis. They found that their manipulation failed to induce the disconfirmatory group to seek disconfirmation. In a follow-up study, Mynatt, Doherty and Tweney (1978) gave subjects more extensive instructions to falsify and rendered the task even more complex yet more realistic by allowing them to explore it in a less constrained manner (e.g., allowing them to design their own experiments instead of forcing them to choose from the potential ones). As in Mynatt *et al.* (1977), however, they found that instructions to disconfirm produced little or no effect on the disconfirmatory group; indeed, 'there was ... almost no indication whatsoever that they (both the disconfirmatory and control groups) intentionally sought disconfirmation' (Mynatt *et al.*, 1978, p. 400). A possible explanation, they suggest, is that a disconfirmatory strategy might simply overload the cognitive capacity of most people—hence the difficulty in eliciting it from them—when they are groping for a means of dealing with complex inference problems. Accordingly, the feasibility of teaching people to falsify seems to depend on whether or not the task is complex.

To complicate matters still further, sometimes it is difficult to judge from the testing behaviour of people whether they have actually followed the falsificatory instruction, for it can be argued that the falsificatory instruction is not carried out successfully if people who are instructed to falsify perform what Wetherick (1962) calls negative tests—i.e. testing their hypothesis by means of test items that it predicts to be false—but at the same time expect the hypothesis to be confirmed rather than falsified by the test result. This argument is echoed and supported by the study of Poletiek (1996), who found that although 60% of subjects in the falsificatory group adopted negative tests, only 10% of them expected a hypothesis-falsifying result, concluding that:

> ... when subjects are asked to behave as falsifiers in a hypothesis-testing task, their behaviour expresses the paradoxical character of this requirement by showing a preference for negative tests on the one hand, but nonetheless expecting this strategy to fail with regard to the production of hypothesis-inconsistent data on the other. (Poletiek, 1996, p. 456)

In other words, it seems 'paradoxical' to regard those who simultaneously use negative tests and expect confirmation of their hypotheses as following the falsificatory instruction. Leaving aside the problem of how to deal with such paradoxical situations that may arise when people are instructed to falsify, an interesting question is: why don't they think and act in the same way? That is, why don't they expect to falsify their hypotheses when performing negative tests? Does it reveal a disbelief at heart in the utility of falsificatory strategies? Do these strategies work in reality?

Should Students Be Taught to Falsify?

Judging from the results of several studies conducted by Michael Gorman and his colleagues in the 1980s, there appear to be grounds for cautious optimism about the utility of falsification. To begin with, in the afore-mentioned study of how different strategies affect the performance of groups in the task adapted from 'New Eleusis' (in Experiment 2), Gorman *et al.* (1984) found that disconfirmatory groups solved significantly more rules (72%) than combined (50%) and confirmatory (25%) groups. Together with the findings that disconfirmatory groups played the highest percentage of incorrect cards (41%) while combined and confirmatory groups played the middle (33%) and the lowest (20%) percentage respectively, and that the percentage of incorrect cards played by these three different groups was highly correlated with their success in solving the rules, this would indicate that the strategy instructions were carried out successfully and indeed accounted for the differences in performance: hence the effectiveness of disconfirmation in problem-solving.

Considering that scientists do not work in error-free environments, in order to model the role of disconfirmation in scientific inference more authentically, Gorman (1986) added the possibility of error to the 'New Eleusis' experiment in another study (with a design virtually identical to the preceding study): subjects were told that 0–20% of the feedback on their trials from the experimenter might be in error, that is, a card that should be correct would be classified as incorrect and vice versa. He found that disconfirmatory groups did not perform significantly better than confirmatory or control (i.e. no-strategy) groups, because the possibility of error interfered with the ability of disconfirmatory groups to obtain and use disconfirmatory information in the sense that it allowed them to immunize their hypotheses against disconfirmation by classifying disconfirmatory information as error, and that it made them spend so much time checking potential errors that they failed to test their hypotheses adequately. However, this result does not mean the futility of disconfirmation under possible-error conditions. Given that the few successful groups used a strategy that combined disconfirmation with replication (i.e. replicating situations in which they thought an error might have occurred), it would imply that disconfirmation becomes even more important as a necessary, though not sufficient, strategy (ibid.).

A Favourable Condition for Disconfirmation to Be Effective

Gorman and Gorman (1984) showed further that the positive effect of disconfirmatory instructions found by Gorman *et al.* (1984) could be replicated on Wason's (1960) 2-4-6 task with individual subjects. Specifically, they found that a significantly larger number of disconfirmatory subjects (95%) than confirmatory (48%) and control (53%) subjects solved the original rule (i.e., 'any three numbers in ascending order') of the task. Curiously enough, such positive effects of disconfirmation on performance did not appear in the afore-mentioned study by Tweney *et al.* (1980), the Experiment 1 of which used a design very similar to Gorman and Gorman's and found that 'while subjects did learn to seek disconfirmatory data, the possession of such strategies led neither to faster solutions, nor to a greater proportion of subjects with correct solutions' (p. 112). Later on, Gorman and his colleagues discovered that the difference between their results and those of Tweney *et al.* was probably caused by the fact that their subjects were given no feedback on the correctness of their guesses until the experiment was over, but Tweney *et al.*'s subjects were informed whether or not each of their guesses about the rule was correct and thus could rely on the experimenter for confirmation or disconfirmation (Gorman, 1992). Therefore, it appears that disconfirmation might be an effective heuristic when people cannot appeal to an outside authority to ascertain whether they are making progress towards a discovery.

Yet, if disconfirmation is less useful when people can appeal to such an authority, then it has little value in the case of laboratory exercises done in many high school and college classes, for, according to Gorman (1995), the objective of most of these exercises is to get the correct answer rather than to explore a novel phenomenon, and frequent appeals to authority in the form of the laboratory assistant or the instructor are not only possible but likely to be helpful. The educational implication is that another, more open-ended and exploratory kind of exercise might provide better training in the use of disconfirmation for future scientists who typically cannot appeal to any authority to test their hypotheses.

The Limits of Disconfirmation

Disconfirmation seems, however, not to be a universally effective strategy for solving reasoning problems. This is substantiated by the results of some 2–4-6 studies (e.g. Gorman & Gorman, 1984; Gorman, Stafford & Gorman, 1987) indicating that it does not work on very general, or more difficult, rules such as 'no two numbers can be the same'. Disconfirmation seems, moreover, not to be self-sufficient either, because sometimes its utility is dependent upon confirmation in two senses. First, strategically, confirmation acts as a necessary complement to disconfirmation, especially in the early stages of a complex inference task. Here are two illustrative examples: Mynatt, Doherty and Tweney (1978) found that although no subjects solved their demanding task, the most successful one initially concentrated on accumulating confirmatory evidence for his hypothesis without regard to disconfirmatory evidence and only sought to establish whether disconfirmatory instances could be found after a relatively well-confirmed hypothesis had been developed; and Karmiloff-Smith and Inhelder (1975) found that young children presented with difficult reasoning problems were incapable of using disconfirmatory evidence—i.e. recognizing counterexamples— until after their hypotheses had been sufficiently confirmed. Echoing the findings of these two studies, Vartanian, Martindale and Kwiatkowski (2003) showed that reliance on a mixed strategy of confirmation and disconfirmation in the early and later stages of hypothesis-testing respectively appeared to be quite advantageous. In fact, in order to defend Faraday against the charge that his deliberate neglect of the disconfirmatory experiments (conducted in 1831 as part of his discovery of electromagnetic induction) reflected a confirmation bias on his part, Tweney and Chitwood (1995) argue instead that what Faraday had done simply manifested a sophisticated use of such a 'confirm early, disconfirm late' strategy, and explained in detail that:

> Nature is chaotic in its character and will frequently provide false feedback to the inquirer. ... [M]any of the experiments tried by Faraday were in fact producing the expected effects but the effects were small and could not be detected with [his] insensitive apparatus. The task of the scientist in such an environment is to impose order on the apparent disorder. ... [O]ne of the necessary functions of a confirmation heuristic ... [is that] it filters out some of the noise and may allow a signal to be detected. This is not a sure thing, which is why a disconfirmatory strategy is a necessary supplement later on. (Tweney & Chitwood, 1995, p. 255)

Second, essentially, a confirmatory strategy not only does not necessarily contradict the goal of seeking disconfirmation, but may be the only way to achieve it in some circumstances. To understand this, according to Klayman and Ha (1987), a confirmatory strategy is better interpreted as a *positive test strategy*, which means testing a hypothesis by examining instances where the target property is hypothesized to be present or is known to be present. Further, it is crucial to distinguish between two different senses of 'seeking disconfirmation'. One sense, which is the focus of empirical investigations, is to examine instances that are predicted not to have the target property, or to conduct negative tests. The other sense, which is emphasized by Popper, is to examine instances that are most expected to falsify the hypothesis. Using Wason's (1960) 2-4-6 task as an example, Klayman and Ha demonstrate graphically that although a positive test strategy cannot produce falsifications in the Popperian sense when the hypothesized rule (e.g. 'increasing by 2') is embedded within the correct rule (e.g. 'increasing numbers', as in Wason's original task), it can do so when the hypothesized rule (e.g. 'increasing by 2') overlaps the correct rule (e.g. 'three even numbers'). More importantly, indeed paradoxically, a positive test strategy is the sole strategy that can reveal conclusive falsifications—even negative tests cannot do so—when the hypothesized rule (e.g. 'increasing by 2') surrounds the correct rule (e.g. 'consecutive even numbers'). We can thus conclude that it is impossible to judge the effectiveness of a confirmatory or positive test strategy in the absence of information about the nature of the task at hand.

Conclusion

To sum up: the implementation of Popper's falsificationist epistemology means exposing to criticism various philosophical presuppositions that work against criticism, including the doctrine that truth is manifest, the demand for precision in concepts as a prerequisite for criticism, essentialism, instrumentalism, and conventionalism; it also means combating the confirmation bias through such educational means as helping teachers and students to acquire an awareness of its pervasiveness and various guises, teaching them to think of several alternative hypotheses simultaneously in seeking explanation of phenomena, encouraging them to assess evidence objectively in the formation and evaluation of hypotheses, and cultivating in them an appropriate attitude towards inconsistent data. With regard to the feasibility of teaching students to falsify, it appears high if teachers adopt relatively simple inference tasks, while creating an opportunity for students to collaborate with each other and lowering the normativity of the learning environment. As for the utility of doing so, although disconfirmation might be an effective heuristic when students cannot appeal to an outside authority to test their hypotheses, it appears not to be a universally effective strategy for solving reasoning problems. In contrast, confirmation seems not to be completely counterproductive and might be a useful heuristic, especially in the early stages of solving by hypothesis a complex inference problem. After all, whether disconfirmation or confirmation is better often depends on the characteristics of the specific task at hand.

References

Baron, J. (1995) Myside Bias in Thinking About Abortion, *Thinking and Reasoning*, 7, pp. 221–235.

Butera, F., Caverni, J.-P. & Rossi, S. (2005) Interaction With a High-Versus Low-Competence Influence Source in Inductive Reasoning, *The Journal of Social Psychology*, 145, pp. 173–190.

Dawson, E., Gilovich, T. & Regan, D. T. (2002) Motivated Reasoning and Performance on the Wason Selection Task, *Personality and Social Psychology Bulletin*, 28, pp. 1379–1387.

Einhorn, H. J. & Hogarth, R. M. (1978) Confidence in Judgment: Persistence of the illusion of validity, *Psychological Review*, 85, pp. 395–416.

Evans, J. St. B. T. (1989) *Bias in Human Reasoning: Causes and consequences* (Hillsdale, NJ, Erlbaum).

Fodor, J. D., Fodor, J. A. & Garrett, M. F. (1975) The Psychological Unreality of Semantic Representations, *Linguistic Inquiry*, 4, pp. 515–531.

Friedrich, J. (1993) Primary Error Detection and Minimization (PEDMIN) Strategies in Social Cognition: A reinterpretation of confirmation bias phenomena, *Psychological Review*, 100, pp. 298–319.

Fugelsang, J. A., Stein, C. B., Green, A. E. & Dunbar, K. N. (2004) Theory and Data Interactions of the Scientific Mind: Evidence from the molecular and the cognitive laboratory,
Canadian Journal of Experimental Psychology, 58, pp. 86–95.

Gardner, M. (1977) On Playing New Eleusis, the Game That Stimulates the Search for Truth,
Scientific American, 237:4, pp. 18–25.

Gorman, M. E. (1986) How the Possibility of Error Affects Falsification on a Task That Models
Scientific Problem Solving, *British Journal of Psychology*, 77, pp. 85–96.

Gorman, M. E. (1992) Experimental Simulations of Falsification, in: M. T. Keane & K. J.
Gilhooly (eds), *Advances in the Psychology of Thinking*, vol. 1 (London, Harvester Wheat-
sheaf), pp. 147–176.

Gorman, M. E. (1995) Hypothesis Testing, in: S. E. Newstead & J. St. B. T. Evans (eds),
Perspectives on Thinking and Reasoning: Essays in honour of Peter Wason (Hove, East Sussex,
Lawrence Erlbaum Associates Ltd.), pp. 217–240.

Gorman, M. E. & Gorman, M. E. (1984) A Comparison of Disconfirmatory, Confirmatory and
Control Strategies on Wason's 2–4–6 Task, *The Quarterly Journal of Experimental Psychology*,
36A, pp. 629–648.

Gorman, M. E., Gorman, M. E., Latta, R. M. & Cunningham, G. (1984) How Disconfirmatory,
Confirmatory and Combined Strategies Affect Group Problem Solving, *British Journal of
Psychology*, 75, pp. 65–79.

Gorman, M. E., Stafford, A. & Gorman, M. E. (1987) Disconfirmation and Dual Hypotheses
on a More Difficult Version of Wason's 2–4–6 Task, *Quarterly Journal of Experimental
Psychology*, 39A, pp. 1–28.

Greenwald, A. G. (1980) The Totalitarian Ego: Fabrication and revision of personal history,
American Psychologist, 35, pp. 603–618.

Hayek, F. A. (1952) *The Sensory Order: An inquiry into the foundations of theoretical psychology*
(London, Routledge & Kegan Paul Ltd.).

Henrion, M. & Fischhoff, B. (1986) Assessing Uncertainty in Physical Constants, *American
Journal of Physics*, 54, pp. 791–798.

Karmiloff-Smith, A. & Inhelder, B. (1975) If You Want to Get Ahead, Get a Theory, *Cognition*,
3, pp. 195–212.

Klayman, J. & Ha, Y.-W. (1987) Confirmation, Disconfirmation, and Information in Hypothesis
Testing, *Psychological Review*, 94, pp. 211–228.

Mahoney, M. J. & Kimper, T. P. (1976) From Ethics to Logics: A survey of scientists, in: M. J.
Mahoney, *Scientist as Subject: The psychological imperative* (Cambridge, MA, Ballinger
Publishing Company), pp. 187–193.

Matlin, M. W. & Stang, D. J. (1978) *The Pollyanna Principle: Selectivity in language, memory and
thought* (Cambridge, MA, Shenkman).

Moshman, D. & Geil, M. (1998) Collaborative Reasoning: Evidence for collective rationality,
Thinking and Reasoning, 4, pp. 231–248.

Mynatt, C. R., Doherty, M. E. & Tweney, R. D. (1977) Confirmation Bias in a Simulated
Research Environment: An experimental study of scientific inference, *Quarterly Journal of
Experimental Psychology*, 29, pp. 85–95.

Mynatt, C. R., Doherty, M. E. & Tweney, R. D. (1978) Consequences of Confirmation and
Disconfirmation in a Simulated Research Environment, *Quarterly Journal of Experimental
Psychology*, 30, pp. 395–406.

Nickerson, R. S. (1998) Confirmation Bias: A ubiquitous phenomenon in many guises, *Review
of General Psychology*, 2, pp. 175–220.

Poletiek, F. H. (1996) Paradoxes of Falsification, *The Quarterly Journal of Experimental Psychology*,
49A, pp. 447–462.

Polya, G. (1954) *Mathematics and Plausible Reasoning: Induction and analogy in mathematics*, vol. 1
(Princeton, NJ, Princeton University Press).

Popper, K. R. (1966) *The Open Society and Its Enemies: The high tide of prophecy*, 5th edn. vol. 2
(London, Routledge).

Popper, K. R. (1979) *Objective Knowledge: An evolutionary approach*, rev. edn. (Hong Kong, Oxford University Press).

Popper, K. R. (1980) *The Logic of Scientific Discovery*, 4th edn. (London, Unwin Hyman Ltd.).

Popper, K. R. (1989) *Conjectures and Refutations: The growth of scientific knowledge*, 5th edn. (London, Routledge).

Popper, K. R. (1996) *The Myth of the Framework: In defence of science and rationality* (London, Routledge).

Popper, K. R. (2002a) *The Poverty of Historicism* (London, Routledge).

Popper, K. R. (2002b) *Unended Quest: An intellectual autobiography*, 2nd edn. (London, Routledge).

Price, D. J. de S. (1963) *Little Science, Big Science* (New York, Columbia University Press).

Pyszczynski, T. & Greenberg, J. (1987) Toward an Integration of Cognitive and Motivational Perspectives on Social Inference: A biased hypothesis-testing model, in: L. Berkowitz (ed.), *Advances in Experimental Social Psychology*, vol. 20 (New York, Academic Press), pp. 297–340.

Sankey, D. (1999) Classrooms as Safe Places to Be Wrong (Paper presented at the UNESCO-ACEID International Conference, Bangkok, Thailand).

Tweney, R. D. (1989) A Framework for the Cognitive Psychology of Science, in: B. Gholson, W. R. Shadish, Jr., R. A. Neimeyer & A. C. Houts (eds), *Psychology of Science* (Cambridge, MA, Cambridge University Press), pp. 342–366.

Tweney, R. D. & Chitwood, S. T. (1995) Scientific Reasoning, in: S. E. Newstead & J. St. B. T. Evans (eds), *Perspectives on Thinking and Reasoning: Essays in honour of Peter Wason* (Hove, East Sussex, Lawrence Erlbaum Associates Ltd.), pp. 241–260.

Tweney, R. D., Doherty, M. E., Worner, W. J., Pliske, D. B., Mynatt, C. R., Gross, K. A. & Arkkelin, D. L. (1980) Strategies of Rule Discovery in an Inference Task, *Quarterly Journal of Experimental Psychology*, 32, pp. 109–123.

Vartanian, O., Martindale, C. & Kwiatkowski, J. (2003) Creativity and Inductive Reasoning: The relationship between divergent thinking and performance on Wason's 2–4–6 task, *The Quarterly Journal of Experimental Psychology*, 56A, pp. 1–15.

Wason, P. C. (1960) On the Failure to Eliminate Hypotheses in a Conceptual Task, *Quarterly Journal of Experimental Psychology*, 12, pp. 129–140.

Wason, P. C. (1961) Response to Affirmative and Negative Binary Statements, *British Journal of Psychology*, 52, pp. 133–142.

Wason, P. C. (1966) Reasoning, in: B. M. Foss (ed.), *New Horizons in Psychology*, vol. 1 (Harmondsworth, England, Penguin), pp. 135–151.

Wetherick, N. E. (1962) Eliminative and Enumerative Behaviour in a Conceptual Task, *Quarterly Journal of Experimental Psychology*, 14, pp. 246–249.

8

Critical Thinking as a Source of Respect for Persons: A critique

CHRISTINE DODDINGTON
University of Cambridge

When we come to consider the nature and purpose of critical thinking, we do not have to go far before we discover its relation to the broader aspiration of rational agency. Together, rationality and critical thinking form 'an ideal appropriate to all education and to all students' (Siegel, 1997, p. 2). The emphasis on rational autonomy in educational aims has resulted in a curriculum and an implied view of personhood that stresses the achievement of certain standards in critical thinking as a priority. For some, this priority extends beyond education with the suggestion that critical thinking has a central value for society itself. 'Making critical thinking a basic aim of our collective educational endeavours in effect grants those endeavours a special status: it establishes education, and its concern for critical thinking, as an independent critic and guide of democratic society' (Siegel, 1988, p. 55).

Before we can examine whether critical thinking is worthy of this central place in our thinking about persons within society, it is important to begin by at least setting out what advocates see as the main characteristics of critical thinking. Critical thinking is broadly seen as the kind of logical thinking that helps us to analyse and make sense of, or interpret, all forms of situations or information so that the conclusions we draw from our interpretations are sound. It is pervasive and is seen as vital to any *developed* life since it entails 'reasonable, reflective thinking that is focused on deciding what to believe and do' (Ennis, 1987, p. 10). There is some debate in the field as to whether critical thinking is generalisable or domain-specific. Some advocates argue that well-considered judgements are the product of general abilities and dispositions while others believe they can only be made within various distinctive disciplines (ethics, science, the arts, for example) and therefore critical thinking and the judgements made will necessarily be by reference to domain-specific criteria. This particular line of argument is then taken to suggest that education needs to encourage the different forms of critical thinking that are embedded in various domains; this in turn has direct consequences for the structure of the school curriculum.

Another distinction that is often made alongside arguments about whether critical thinking should be seen as a set of domain-specific or generalisable skills concerns the limitation of viewing critical thinking as skill alone. 'Along with the skill or ability to assess the probative force of reasons, critical thinkers must also have relevant *dispositions.* The primary disposition consists in valuing good reasoning and being disposed to seek reasons, to assess them and to govern beliefs and actions on the basis of such assessment' (Bailin & Siegel, 2003, p. 183). Critical thinkers are therefore those who *choose* to seek out and critically examine their underlying assumptions and thus consistently evaluate their beliefs and actions. As such, critical thinking is prized not just as an ability, but for incorporating dispositions that give us a particular orientation towards experience and life in general.

It is with this thought that we begin to feel the extent of the comprehensive and universal nature that is being claimed for the role of critical thinking in person-hood. In terms of education, the moves a teacher makes towards strengthening and bettering a student's powers of critical thought can begin from the earliest days of a child's school career. Thus, in an animated discussion with six-year-olds we can see the beginnings of reasoning from which to build towards a justified understanding of the world. As the children discuss the very process of thinking, one child asserts 'If you didn't have a brain, you wouldn't be able to think at all!'. When questioned, he explains that we need our brains, they help us to stand up and think and speak. Across the circle, another child disagrees and claims that it is not with our brains, but with our hearts that we think. Yet another claims that thoughts are quantifiable because 'At the end of the day I sometimes feel that I have used up all my thoughts'. Questioning, disagreement and lively exchanges, claims and counter-claims take the discussion forward with little input from the teacher. In this captured moment we could argue that the powers of critical thinking are already present with a clear capacity for being developed. For many educators, to fully respect each and every child as a person in their own right would be to take each child through the years of their education, sensitively strengthening their capacity for critical thought and gently correcting the naivety of their world view—in short, to induct them into a stance towards the world in which information, problems and experience can be probed to form sound beliefs, decisions and judgements for a flourishing and well-grounded way of life.

Critical thinking has of course been the subject of a number of critiques. According to Bailin and Siegel, some of these attempts to examine critical thinking leave the basic premise of its importance and centrality intact, and in many cases have actually served to refine its theory and practice. This process has resulted in a revised, more comprehensive version of critical thinking. For example, critical thinking is no long seen in contrast to feeling, but can now be seen to include emotion, as long as reason is still seen as primary. Bailin and Siegel suggest that we can now see that sensitivity to other perspectives and other's feelings can become part of what it is to think critically. Furthermore, this kind of thinking can be practised both autonomously and in a collegial and collaborative manner. Finally, critical thinking is not simply linear and deductive, but can have a gener-ative, imaginative component (Bailin & Siegel, 2003, p. 186). Where critiques have not enhanced the overall conception of critical thinking, Bailin and Siegel view them as largely 'misdirected in failing to recognize aspects that already exist in much contemporary critical thinking theory, or are problematic in suggesting revisions that might undermine important aspects of critical thinking (2003, p. 190).

A second kind of critique—that critical thinking is culturally or context specific and therefore only one, and perhaps a rather arbitrary, form of thinking amongst others—is seen as more radical. However, Bailin and Siegel respond to these approaches by acknowledging that human practices and traditions are dynamic and open-ended, and often contain alternative and competing streams of thinking. They go on to point out, however, that any tradition of *rational inquiry* has to be based on principles that are closely tied to purposes, and that this is therefore a universal quality that cannot generate ways of thinking that are simply products of a particular group's interests. Again we are reminded of the sense in which critical thinking is embedded within a view of rationality.

Now, much of this kind of argument is powerful, not least because it exemplifies many of the very criteria associated with rationality and critical thinking. However, the implicit claim that we should revere this as being at the heart of education for personhood and a flourishing life is more troubling. To understand why this is, we need to look more closely at some writers who have articulated alternative views of how we should conceive of being in the world. These alternative views are more fundamental than the claims that alternative ways of thinking are generated for specific contexts or grow from particular groups. They begin to imply that alongside the undeniably useful approach to life and the world that is embraced by critical thinking, there are equally valuable, or even prior, elements of person-hood and a distinctly human relationship to the world that need conceptualising if we are to fully understand what it is to respect and therefore to educate persons.

The concepts of sense, perception and embodiment will be central to what follows, but these ideas cover a vast area far too large to tackle within a single paper. My intention, therefore, is to raise one or two elements that I believe are pertinent to a discussion of critical thinking and that in turn give a flavour of some alternative views of how persons should relate to the world that might offer a contrast to the prevailing views of the centrality of rational thought. We need to begin with one obvious dimension of the legacy of Descartes that impinges on ideas of critical thinking—that a person is mind, but is also body. In the last century there were attempts to re-unify this Cartesian dualism, and from this has grown some interesting work on the neglected role of experience and corporeality in consciousness. I believe that a full acknowledgement of this dimension within an inclusive account of critical thinking has yet to be made.

At a very basic level, many accept the idea that human beings come into existence as live, physical, sensing entities that gradually mature and acquire attributes that make them persons. High on this list of personhood attributes come consciousness, intentionality and other features traditionally associated with mind. However, one challenge to this standard view seeks to explain and evaluate the *continuing* place of spontaneous, physical experience in our development of mind. The argument is that although our minds may be active in any experience of the world, the mind is not just an inner function of the body. Instead, we should acknowledge that we are first and foremost *embodied*, so that mind pervades our corporeal existence and is not somehow added on.

For some writers in this field, the claim that sensing and perceiving is the basis from which we become persons does not mean that the standard account of knowledge as objective is necessarily somehow false. Instead, they point out that our corporeal way of relating to the world is *prior*, and that objectifying and rationalising about the world should be seen as secondary and dependent upon this more fundamental way of encountering the world.

> All my knowledge of the world, even my scientific knowledge, is gained from my own particular point of view, or from some experience of the world without which the symbols of science would be meaningless. The whole universe of science is built upon the world as directly experienced, and if we want to subject science itself to rigorous scrutiny and arrive at a precise assessment of its meaning and scope, we must begin by reawakening the basic experience of the world, of which science is the second-order expression. ... To return to things themselves is to return to that world which precedes knowledge [and] of which knowledge always *speaks*. (Merleau-Ponty, 1962, p. viii)

Or, to put this more succinctly, 'Our spontaneous experience of the world, charged with subjective, emotional, and intuitive content, remains the vital and dark ground of all our objectivity, ... which largely goes unnoticed or unacknowledged in scientific culture' (Abrams, 1996, p. 34).

The tension here is that subjectivity, emotion and intuition feature in the form of encounter with the world that rationality is precisely held to guard against. So what is this living dimension in which all of our endeavours should somehow be rooted, and how do we conceptualise and avoid slippage into atomised subjectivism?

Husserl first tried to identify an element of lived experience that he felt remained ignored by previous accounts of human engagement with the world: he used the term 'life-world' to signal its pervasive significance. For him, the life-world did not arise purely in an *individual's* sensing experience because he was able to see that this would imply a form of solipsism. Instead, Husserl was careful to explain the 'life-world' as an *intersubjective* world of lived experience, pre-theoretical, concretely real, and ultimately shared and imagined beyond a single perspective. On his account, my first glimpse of a teacup placed on a table is augmented by an apprehension that there are other perspectives that I cannot, at that time, physically see. My previous experiences of that and other cups allow me, easily and almost unconsciously, to complete the full roundness of the cup and apprehend its function. Similarly, when I stand with others surrounding and gazing at a tree, I sense there is more to the tree than I can see at that moment, and the perspectives from others around the tree can supplement, enlarge and endorse my view. Husserl, then, saw the world:

> ... not as a sheer 'object' ... from which all subjects and subjective qualities should be pared away, but [as] rather an intertwined matrix of sensations and perceptions, a collective field of experience lived through from many different angles [and] ... sustained by continual encounter

with others, with other embodied subjects, other centres of experience. ...
It is this informing of my perceptions by the evident perceptions and
sensations of other bodily entities that establishes, for me, the relative
solidity and stability of the world. (Abrams, 1996, p. 39)

One argument that could be made here is that Husserl is merely identifying the
socio-cultural dimension of sense-making. However, he seems to be aspiring to
something much more fundamental that lies beneath the diversity of culturally
constructed life-worlds: 'a deeper, more unitary life-world always already there
beneath all our cultural acquisitions' (Abrams, 1996, p. 41). This claim contrasts
strikingly with a rationalist view that the world pre-exists and that it is through the
principled and rule-bound disciplines that we can truly come to know and think
about the world. It would seem that Husserl is indicating a space here for both the
individualised and collective sensing from which reflection should spring. Bearing
this in mind, it is worth looking at other writers, undoubtedly influenced by
Husserl, who explore this idea further.

One aspect of this line of thinking is that it appears to call into question the very
worth of objectivity or at least the version of objectivity and reality that we have
inherited from the Greeks. The notion that for the development of knowledge we
need to become critical cataloguers, calculators, and spectators of the phenomena
that comprise the world has been an accepted western view for centuries. The urge
has been to gain understanding through the disinterested study of objects, others
and ourselves; the argument goes that these substances and their inter-relationships
stand independently of and are prior to our individual experience of them. It is by
analysing and objectifying them that we learn to think critically about the world
and come to know how it is constituted. However, following Husserl, other writers
turn this assumption around. Heidegger, for instance, argued that when we position ourselves over and against objects, we come to view them arrayed and present
before us in a remote way. This way of examining the world serves, it is once again
suggested, to eclipse the primordial relationship that is needed to fully grasp the
meaning of something. For Heidegger, an encounter with something is 'not a bare
perceptual cognition, but ... the kind of concern which manipulates things and puts
them to use; and this has its own kind of "knowledge"' (1962, p. 67). Our awareness
comes through experience or how we deal with the world—how we use things, and
Heidegger argues that this use is given sense by our distinctive human concerns
and projects. To a very real degree, the world is necessarily and primarily a human
world 'whose structure, articulation and very existence are functions of human
agency' (Cooper, 1990, p. 58).

A further dimension of this sense of the world comes from Heidegger's insistence
on the sign-like quality of things we encounter in lived experience. If we return to
the image of the teacup placed on a table, Husserl would draw attention to multiple
viewpoints to augment a single view, but in this example I mentioned the function
of the cup that would enhance my apprehension of it. For Heidegger it is not only
the simple function that a cup serves, but also the significance that it can have in
lived experience and its relationship to other things. The cup can be seen as a sign,

for it carries within it reference to its uses and to other substances (tea, heat, saucer, teapot), as well as drawing forth awareness of previous experiences that give it meaning. Heidegger includes language within this 'sign-like' sense in which we encounter the world. Words cannot be truly understood atomistically through objective definition, but are always encountered in use and are best understood within a web of reference. In practice, words are sounds that gain meaning through human intention and use, and for Heidegger this is the same for substances we encounter in the world. For him, this proximal relationship and intuited sense of a world called into being by the very presence of a simple vessel comprise the thick and rich world of experience that nourishes and draws forth thinking. The extent of corporeality in thinking that Heidegger wishes to draw our attention to is perhaps best illustrated by the following:

> But the craft of the hand is richer than we commonly imagine. The hand does not only grasp and catch, or push and pull. The hand reaches and extends, receives and welcomes—and not just things: the hand extends itself, and receives its own welcome in the hands of others. The hand holds. The hand carries. The hand designs and signs, presumably because man is a sign. Two hands fold into one, a gesture meant to carry man into the great oneness. The hand is all this and this is the true handicraft. Everything is rooted here that is commonly known as handicraft, and commonly we go no further. But the hand's gestures run everywhere through language, in their most perfect purity precisely when man speaks by being silent. And only when man speaks, does he think—not the other way around, as metaphysics still believes. Every motion of the hand in every one of its works carries itself through the element of thinking; every bearing of the hand bears itself in that element. All the work of the hand is rooted in thinking. ... We have called thinking the handicraft *par excellence*. Thinking guides and sustains every gesture of the hand. (Heidegger, 1968, p. 23)

Heidegger seems to be approaching a form of thinking here that is somewhat removed from our accepted idea of critical thinking. Detachment is one aspect that would work against quality of thought in his story: we should instead allow ourselves to be immersed in life, open to the nature of objects and others that surround us. The implication suggested is that the deeper we envelop ourselves, the deeper our capacity to care and the deeper our understanding and quality of thought. For Heidegger, it is not just the distance that is problematic with a form of critical thinking. His work seems to suggest that if we adopt a stance towards the world that is not only distant but also critical or challenging, our relationship and apprehension of the world changes, so that the world and its objects become diminished. Instead of the rich primordial relationship which allows all things to be unconcealed, substances lose their full sensuous weight for us and become levelled and measurable, perhaps even demeaned. Some have argued that this sees Heidegger claiming that all objects, both inanimate and animate, are therefore deserving of dignity that is lost when they become subsumed under the 'mastery' of a human approach that is in denial of the more fundamental relationship (Waddington, 2005, p. 574). We might add here that this 'mastery' and 'challenging approach' could well echo some forms of critical thinking where judgements are made on the basis of information that is objectively gathered and analysed.

Heidegger stresses our relationship with the world in terms of references, usage, concerns and personal projects that inevitably 'colour' our sense and use of elements in the world. Merleau-Ponty too pursues the extent of human involvement and engagement, but calls for closer attention to the bodily sensing and perception that accompanies our experience of being in the world. He argues that the body as the true organ of experience is not just the first way of engagement with the world, but retains its primacy so that the sentient and sensuous body must be at the heart of even our most abstract thinking. If we return to our singular teacup and imagine it with other objects within a room, Merleau-Ponty delicately elaborates the suggestion first found in Husserl to explain how we can make sense within the mêlée of sensual experience:

> [E]ach presence presents some facet that catches my eye while the rest of it lies hidden behind the horizon of my current position, each one inviting me to focus my senses upon it, to let the other objects fall into the background as I enter into its particular depth. (Abrams, 1996, p. 52)

For Merleau-Ponty, then, the body is the means by which we may enter into perspectival relation with all things; to stand above or away from the world to reflect is artificial and can block the living, reverberating activity of the world. Our bodies merge us into the very midst of things, and things perceived merge into us.

> A thing is, therefore, not actually *given* in perception; it is internally taken up by us, reconstituted and experienced by us in so far as it is bound up with a world, the basic structures of which we carry with us, and of which it is merely one of many possible concrete forms. (Merleau-Ponty, 1962, p. 327)

An acknowledgement that objects are 'bound up with a world' and that we carry the basic structures of that world with us seems to be the primal way in which we make sense from experience. This means that human encounter in all its forms should be seen as a dynamic, sensual and reciprocal activity requiring openness and creative participation—an active interplay between the perceiver and the perceived. Donn Welton expresses something of the contrast this gives with our standard account of approaching the world. Following Husserl, all objects are to be understood as lived objects long before they become objects for critical thought. He explains that scientific characterisation:

> ... is derived, with the ringing surfaces of the cobblestones on which I walk, with the rough board I am planing, with the supple face I embrace and hold in my hands. Surfaces that support, boards that are planed, faces that are embraced; they have an 'aesthetic' extension and then a flesh,

one that our perceptions enfold, that is not yet the result of a categorical synthesis, of an act of cognition or, better, interpretation. (Welton, 1999, p. 53)

A further consideration is needed before we return to the questions concerning personhood, education and critical thinking that were raised at the beginning of this paper. It might be possible to accept the descriptions offered to us of a life world and embodied existence, to acknowledge that they alert us to fundamental ways of interacting with each other and the world itself, but where does this take us? To some extent these descriptions can be seen (perhaps due to my characterisation) as somewhat passive—an indulgent, sensual wallow perhaps? Critical thinking at least gives us a strong sense of direction towards conclusions and judgements, so how should we understand a basic human movement *towards* the world that is not detached, critical or rational?

In the account I am trying to set out, the main dynamic comes from what David Cooper calls the existential sense of 'directives' that lend shape to a person's life. These are the personal beliefs, concerns, values and interpretations seen not as features of character, but as something deeper and more binding—the very sense in which aspects of the world and our living have *meaning* and come to matter to us (Cooper, 1990, p. 114). If we are to support children into true understanding rather than information acquisition under the guise of knowledge, some educationalists argue that there is a pressing need to take account of these 'directives'. In his book, *Children's Thinking*, Michael Bonnett finds the rationalist perspective's ambition to give an account of the whole of thinking contentious because of:

... its lack of appreciation of the importance of 'subjective weight' in a person's understanding and general mode of relating to things, and its consequent overlooking of the role played by a person's own motivations in the meanings they are able to achieve in their thinking. (Bonnett, 1996, p. 97)

The notion of 'directives' and the 'subjective weight' they give seem again to be the very same aspects that we are advised should be stripped from our judgement as we struggle towards the objectivity required of critical thinking.

Despite extensive differences in the two or three views I have briefly sketched, I believe there are some common areas that emerge when we consider the arguments pertinent to our concerns here. The attack on detached, critical thought implies that it is a secondary form of thinking that has some value but that this value is limited. In particular, analytical thinking, with its emphasis on calculative judgement, can work against and take us away from the sense of ourselves as embodied and embedded in the world. (Perhaps this idea is the spring for Leonardo da Vinci's reported aphorism that 'intellectuality drives out sensuality'?) For an education concerned with developing persons and encouraging a flourishing life the implications seem profound. If thought and feeling ultimately make sense only through our continued physical engagement and meaning-making with the world, then understanding the nature of this engagement becomes a priority and the form that education then takes should acknowledge and reflect this understanding.

For Bonnett, the notion of challenging and calculative thinking can be set distinctly against the notion of poetic or meditative thinking that Heidegger develops. Bonnett's book is a call for the curriculum to redress the imbalance that has resulted from the dominance of the rationalist perspective in education. His summary of the contrasting features of poetic and calculative thinking is perhaps the best way to highlight this. He first sets out a table to illustrate the two different stances:

Calculative	*Poetic*
Self-purposeful	Celebratory
Goal-oriented	Openly curious, wondering
Analyses things into problems	Intuits the wholeness of things
to be solved	and receives them as they are
Turns things into defined objects	Stays with things in their inherent
—manageable, familiar	strangeness

He then distinguishes the feelings and aspirations of each way of thinking:

Calculative	*Poetic*
Satisfaction as a result of sense of	Sense of mystery, awe, wonder, fascination
sorting things out, getting things	evokes feelings of attunement
ordered, made clear, transparent	
Effects things	Affected by things
Seeks control	Allows itself to be vulnerable
Makes statements	'Sings', 'says' what is
Seeks truth as correctness	Seeks truth as revealing

Distinctions made in this way serve to illustrate something of the limitations of critical thinking. I am aware that one way of challenging this conceptualisation of a dualist approach to kinds of thinking would be to argue that critical thinking in its full sense is not equitable to the calculative thinking that Bonnett describes; or, alternatively, maybe a richer notion of critical thought would allow for some of the dimensions that Heidegger wishes to attach to a poetic relationship with the world. The problem with this latter line of argument is that I believe it blurs the notion of critical thinking, stretching it too far so that it has little use for those who need to conceptualise and articulate it in the practice of education. It seems to me that Merleau-Ponty, Heidegger and others have made distinctions that help to retrieve neglected dimensions of human existence and that these distinctions seem particularly valuable when we consider how we should come to respect children and what it is for them to develop personhood. For this reason, the kind of polarisation offered by Bonnett is helpful, for it allows these overlooked dimensions of being to come to the fore as we think about the nature of education.

If we return to the classroom of six-year-olds and imagine the natural orientation for an educator wedded to the centrality of critical thinking, her aim would be ultimately to help the children come to a correct view of what thinking is. The endearing comment that we think with our hearts would, at some stage, have to be replaced through critical, scientific knowledge by a more accurate understanding, and to pursue this would be seen as a mark of the respect that educator had for that child. An educator influenced by a commitment to the alternative view I have articulated might have a different perspective. The 'correct' view about the function of the heart would be less important than the strength and source of this child's present belief, drawn deeply (for it is made with great conviction) from her personal experience of the world. To respect her in this view would allow her teacher to respond and create an education in which, for example, senses and perceptions could be cherished and strengthened, beliefs could be taken seriously and explored, and expression of genuine concerns, things that matter, could be encouraged.

It would be absurd to suggest that this form of education should eradicate the more traditional view that highlights the value of objective knowledge and the critical thought in which this knowledge is based. My argument is simply that a view that *over-valorises* critical thinking at the expense of other aspects of humanity results in a reduced and therefore distorting view of what we should value and cherish about personhood through education, and may also mislead us in forming the substance and priority of what should be in the curriculum. It is, perhaps, easiest to see and address this distortion within early years education, and I suspect that many educators experienced in this field would have sympathy with the thrust of my arguments and the illustrations I have provided. However, my intention is also to suggest that these ideas have relevance beyond a particular age phase.

I have used the work of other writers to suggest alternative ways of thinking that might be important for the education of persons. Where logical distinctions can be made, they point not to a distinct form of thinking that is completely 'other' than critical thinking, but to a form of thinking that diminishes the significance of a rational emphasis in favour of a more contemplative, open, even loving orientation towards others and the world. We begin life utterly embodied and drowned in sensation, and the assumption that we should move away from this towards mindful objectivity is deeply ingrained in our view of education. This seems to have become a denial of the full richness of personhood that education should address. The ability to savour and consciously conceptualise our experiences without introducing the force of critical analysis can also qualify as 'good' thinking if the criteria we use to judge what is good include developing our sense of personhood and well being. Perhaps we should begin to redress this balance by renaming this perspective 'personal' as opposed to 'critical' thinking. Personal thinking might then be defended as the basis from which, for example, we are able to form strong, well-grounded kinds of relationships to the world, others and even ourselves. On this story, critical thinking would become a further embellishment to be used as and when appropriate rather than the fundamental basis for our orientation to the world and our way of living.

If education is to address the kinds of person that we are to become, we need a curriculum that relishes and makes full recognition of the richness and primacy of sense, perception and embodied personal thinking. All these features cannot be subsumed into critical thought. Instead, we require education to be connected with this fundamental sentient-base of how we exist and become persons. There is not space here to elaborate fully the educational implications of a shift towards personal thinking as I have introduced it, but I hope I have shown that to educate a thinking person cannot, and should not, be just about educating him or her to think critically. In this we show respect for the whole person, and not just for the person who has developed the capacity for rationally based critical thought.

References

Abrams, D. (1996) *The Spell of the Sensuous* (New York, Pantheon Books).

Bailin, S. & Siegel, H. (2003) Critical Thinking, in: N. Blake, P. Smeyers, R. Smith & P. Standish (eds), *The Blackwell Guide to the Philosophy of Education* (Oxford, Blackwell).

Bonnett, M. (1994) *Children's Thinking. Promoting understanding in the primary school* (London, Cassell).

Cooper, D. (1990) *Existentialism* (Oxford, Blackwell).

Ennis, R. H. (1987) A Taxonomy of Critical Thinking Dispositions and Abilities, in: J. Boykoff-Baron & R. J. Sternberg (eds), *Teaching Thinking Skills: Theory and pactice* (New York, W. H. Freeman), p. 10.

Heidegger, M. (1962) *Being and Time* (Oxford, Blackwell).

Heidegger, M. (1968) *What is Called Thinking* (New York, Harper and Row).

Merleau-Ponty, M. (1962) *Phenomenology of Perception* (London, Routledge & Kegan Paul).

Siegel, H. (1988) *Educating Reason: Rationality, Critical Thinking and Education* (New York, Routledge).

Siegel, H. (1997) *Rationality Redeemed? Further dialogues on an educational ideal* (New York, Routledge).

Waddington, D. (2005) A Field Guide to Heidegger: Understanding 'The Question concerning Technology', *Educational Philosophy and Theory*, 37:4.

Welton, D. (1999) Soft, Smooth Hands, in: D. Welton (ed.), *The Body* (Oxford, Blackwell).

9

Re-conceptualizing Critical Thinking for Moral Education in Culturally Plural Societies

DUCK-JOO KWAK
Konkuk University, Korea

Introduction

There have in the last two or three decades been various lines of criticism from postmodern and feminist perspectives of the prevailing conception of critical thinking and its justification as a primary aim of education. Even if its status as one of the primary aims of education has not been completely undermined, the concept and its justification as an educational aim have been under serious pressure.[1] The attacks appear to be directed primarily at the Cartesian sense of rationality on which the concept of critical thinking is based. This Cartesian rationality is criticized for privileging rational and linear thought over intuition, and for neglecting emotions and lived experiences from concrete situations (Kohli, 1995, p. 83). It is considered to politically exclude historically marginalized or oppressed groups by posing a universal standard of rationality as the formal procedure of thinking. In other words, this unfavourable attitude to critical thinking today derives mainly from a morally motivated aspiration for inclusion.

However, in a solidly sustained defence of critical thinking, modernist educators such as Robert Ennis and Harvey Siegel try to redefine the concept of critical thinking in a broader sense. Ennis defines critical thinking as 'reasonable reflective thinking that is focused on deciding what to believe and do', whereas Siegel describes it as an ability to judge in such a way as to meet 'relevant standards or criteria of acceptability' (Blake *et al.*, 2003, p. 181). Although also opposing the exclusion of historically marginalized or oppressed groups, they are still concerned with epistemic criteria or standards that reason must meet in order to be judged good reasons, namely, reasons that warrant beliefs, claims, and actions. Thus, they counterattack their critics by asking them how they can coherently criticize the oppression or marginalization of particular groups without appealing to rational criteria that transcend cultural, social or gender-based boundaries. Their worry is that, if we do not have such criteria, we would be easily led into a relativism of rationality in public discourse, as different people have different ideas about what it is to be rational.

To revisit critical thinking as one of the primary aims of education requires that we take seriously the respective concerns of both sides, as well as what is shared by them. The postmodern detractors from critical thinking seem to be interested in the question of how we can *coexist* or even *flourish with* differences and conflicts among those with different cultural, religious, or racial backgrounds, while the modernist advocates are concerned with the question of how the differences or conflicts can be *rationally resolved*. The former stress our disposition to be open-minded, to bring into public discourse more voices from diverse groups; the latter prioritize finding more objective knowledge of what to believe and procedures as to how to act in the public arena. Despite these differences, however, both sides appear to share a *moral* concern, i.e. opposition to the injustice of excluding historically marginalized or oppressed groups. So I wonder if there might be a new way of conceptualizing critical thinking in such a way as to accommodate both concerns, modern and postmodern, especially in the context of moral education today. The clarification of the nature of critical thinking and its role in moral education, especially in terms of its contributions and its limitations, may lead us into a better position to do so. I find an important clue to embark on this endeavour in Bernard Williams's view on the limits of philosophy-as-justificatory power for ethics.

Williams puts forward two (postmodern) assumptions about the nature of ethics. One is that ethical knowledge of what is right or wrong, if there is such a thing, is not *necessarily* the best *ethical state*.[2] The other is that 'in the process of losing ethical knowledge (which we have already acquired), we may gain knowledge of other kinds, about human nature, history, what the world actually is like' (1985, p. 168). The first assumption indicates that the attainment of ethical knowledge, that is, rationally justifiable ethical belief, may not be sufficient for moral education; so this assumption provides us with a critical stance from which we might see the limitations of the modernist advocacy of a view of critical thinking that prioritizes epistemic criteria to achieve rationally justifiable knowledge. On the other hand, the second assumption implies that ethical knowledge is still worth obtaining since a process of losing it might bring to us other kinds of knowledge. Williams later describes these other kinds of knowledge as the *understanding* of the ethical, as opposed to ethical knowledge. Thus, the second assumption will be useful in alleviating the postmodern and feminist attacks on critical thinking and redirecting the attacks more fruitfully.

Taking Williams's two assumptions as guiding principles, this paper aims to offer a fruitful way of re-conceptualizing critical thinking in moral education. To do so, I will first critically examine two earlier views on critical thinking, Siegel's as modern and Burbules's as postmodern, as a way to a new formulation of critical thinking in moral education. Then I will argue for Williams's formulation of critical thinking in moral education, centring on his concept of ethical reflection, which seems to be more suitable for culturally pluralistic societies.

A Critical Review of Two Earlier Approaches to Critical Thinking, Modern and Postmodern

What is critical thinking? Modernist theorists conceive of it in terms of both the ability and the disposition to critically evaluate beliefs, their underlying assumptions, and the worldviews in which those beliefs are embedded. Siegel (1988, p. 23) emphasizes not only the critical thinker's mastery of 'epistemic criteria' that reasons must meet in order to be rightly judged to be good reasons that warrant beliefs, claims, and actions, but also their tendency to be 'appropriately moved by reasons,' i.e. a tendency to be open-minded, fair-minded, and respectful of others in deliberation. However, it is important to notice that, even while emphasizing equally these two components of critical thinking, Siegel also makes it clear that they are conceptually distinct and have different priorities in constituting the concept of critical thinking. Contrasting epistemic criteria with epistemic virtues, he argues (1997, p. 107, p. 172) that only the former can determine whether a belief is justified, whereas the latter merely increases the likelihood that an inquiry leads to a rational outcome. Here we can see that Siegel takes the role of epistemic virtues in critical thinking as limited and secondary, in the sense of holding that how much open-mindedness or willingness to listen to others is to be allowed should be determined by epistemic criteria as 'relevant standards or criteria of acceptability' that transcend particular social circumstances.

There are two things to be drawn from Siegel's view. One is that, by adding the second component of epistemic virtue, Siegel seems to suggest that critical thinking has to do with a feature of one's *character*. The other is that, if it is a character feature, it is so only in a very thin sense because it has to do with one's disposition to subject oneself to epistemic criteria, which are *external to* oneself, i.e. to one's beliefs and desires. This implies that critical thinking is a disposition to stand back in rational reflection from one's own beliefs and desires, which is concerned with *truth* or *justice*. And critical deliberation about the true or the just employs a standpoint that is impartial and seeks harmony as part of epistemic criteria. But this *impartial* attitude will not usually be shared by our reflective deliberation on what to do in the moral domain. For in our reflective deliberation in the moral domain, the *I* that stands back in rational reflection from one's desires is still the *I* that has those desires and will empirically act; here radical self-detachment like impartiality is not necessarily required as in critical thinking. Thus, by being able simply to stand back from one's desire in reflection, one is not converted into someone whose fundamental interest lies in the harmony of all beliefs or all interests. In other words, just taking this step of standing back from one's desire cannot result in us acquiring the motivations to truth or justice.

Thus, while rightly holding that critical thinking requires a particular kind of character feature, i.e. a critical spirit of self-detachment in the form of impartiality, Siegel fails to offer an account of how it can be acquired in such a way as to be consistent with the personhood that consists of one's interests in life. In other words, his account of critical thinking lacks an account of what it is to take an impartial perspective, while still being in touch with enough identity of one's own to live a life that respects one's own interests.[3] I think this is the real cause of the problem in teaching critical thinking in the moral realm, where we often see in the college classroom that students who are good at critical thinking often lack the ability to reflect on their *own* beliefs and desires, which is closely connected to the ethical dimension of their lives.

On the other hand, Siegel takes critical thinking as something *general* manifested in any good thinking rather than as domain- or context-specific, 'emphasizing the generalizability of abilities constitutive of critical thinking' (Bailin & Siegel, 2003, p. 185). This means that he tends not to make a distinction between science and morality in the nature of critical thinking. I think that this is mistaken. To illustrate my point, let me quote Socrates' dialogue in the *Euthyphro* as a relevant instance:

Socrates:	What are the subjects of difference that cause hatred and anger? Let us look at it this way. If you and I were to differ about numbers as to which is the greater, would this difference make us enemies and angry with each other, or would we proceed to count and soon resolve our difference about this?
Euthyphro:	We would certainly do so.
Socrates:	Again, if we differed about the larger and the smaller, we would turn to measurement and soon cease to differ.
Euthyphro:	That is so.
Socrates:	And about the heavier and the lighter, we would resort to weighing and be reconciled.
Euthyphro:	Of course.
Socrates:	What subject of difference would make us angry and hostile to each other if we were unable to come to a decision? Perhaps you do not have an answer ready, but examine as I tell you whether these subjects are the just and the unjust, the beautiful and the ugly, the good and the bad. Are these not the subjects of difference about which, when we are unable to come to a satisfactory decision, you and I and other men become hostile to each other whenever we do? (Plato, 1981, p. 11)

The above dialogue seems to tell us two things about the nature of *moral arguments*, which can be taken as a mode of critical thinking. One is that it is natural that we end up with quarrels when making moral arguments. The other is that this is because moral arguments in their nature differ from arguments in science and mathematics; unlike the latter, the former is usually incapable of rational settlement. But, I think modernist educators like Siegel would be likely to reject both points by assuming that *the rationality* of moral argument depends upon its leading from premises all parties accept, in steps all can follow, to an agreement upon a conclusion which all must accept. For them, the goal of moral argument is in principle agreement upon a conclusion concerning what ought to be done, and any disagreement can be resolved by epistemic criteria as 'relevant standards or criteria of acceptability' that transcend the particular social circumstances. Thus, they would take 'ending up with quarrel' in itself as the evidence of incompetence in critical thinking on the part of the engaged, incompetence which is susceptible to moral relativism.

However, if two cultures or two moral outlooks differ from one another, someone who has certain dispositions and expectations as a member of one culture will, when confronted with an alternative moral outlook, often be unwilling to see or do what is done in the other culture. It is part of what makes his or her response an *ethical* response that he or she has deeply internalized enough for this reaction of not mere unwillingness, but in some cases, rejection of the alternatives. For this unwillingness or rejection has to do with a common phenomenon that the ethical thought of any given culture tends to stretch beyond the boundary of its own culture and claims its universality. In other words, the fact that we easily end up with quarrels over moral issues derives from the nature of ethical thought. But, as Williams (1985, p. 159) points out, this nature of ethical thought may not be about the objectivity of the ethical thought, but about its content or aspiration. This means that, even if there is no way in which divergent ethical beliefs can be brought to converge with one another by rational argument or independent inquiry, each moral outlook may still make claims that it intends to apply to the whole world, not just to that part of it which is its own. That is to say, the fact of no rational settlement of moral arguments, or non-objectivity of moral beliefs, does not necessarily imply a relativistic attitude on the part of the moral agent, and nor does it lead him or her into a state of relativism, as Siegel worries; it is rather part of the nature of moral argument.

Thus, my dissatisfaction with Siegel's theory of critical thinking is twofold. One is the lack of a solid account of the character feature of critical thinking, namely, how the *I* who has taken the perspective of impartiality can coexist with enough identity to live a life that respects one's own interests. The other is with his excessive concern with relativism. I have shown that the fact of no rational settlement in moral arguments does not necessarily lead us as moral agents into relativism since our ethical thinking still *in its nature* aspires to its universal application, if not to its objectivity.

Sceptical, not dismissive, of Siegel's concept of critical thinking, the moderate postmodern thinker Nicholas Burbules comes up with a modified concept of rationality, namely, 'reasonableness'. In contrast to Siegel's concept of critical thinking which is based on rationality as the formal and universal criterion of thought to which everyone is expected to conform, Burbules's concept of reasonableness refers to the dispositions and capacities of a certain kind of person, 'a person who is related in specific contexts to other persons, not to the following of formal rules and procedures of thought' (1995, pp. 85–6). What should be noted is that 'the dispositions and capacities of a certain kind of person' seems to mean *more* than the mere combination of the skills of logical reasoning and the disposition to be appropriately moved by reasons. While describing reasonableness as a more complex set of features of any reflective thought in relation to others, Burbules attributes it to the character of a person who is capable of applying the skills of logical reasoning in a specific context of practice. In other words, Burbules characterizes reasonableness as 'virtues' that are related to one's sense of self or integrity as flexible aspects of character. Thus, Burbules's reasonableness can be taken as a complex set of *epistemic virtues*, epistemic in the sense that it is a feature of any reflective thought, and virtues in the sense that they are aspects of one's character. Burbules (ibid., p. 86) thus portrays a reasonable person as someone who 'wants to make sense, wants to be fair to alternative points of view, and wants to be careful and prudent in the adoption of important positions in life, and willing to admit when he or she has made a mistake', as well as knowing how and when he or she should change his or her mind.

If we formulate the concept of critical thinking in terms of Burbules's reasonableness, it would have two distinctive features. First, critical thinking would be closely related to the ethical formation of one's selfhood: the primary concern in critical thinking education would be the examination of one's own desires and actions in relation to others', rather than vice versa. Second, critical thinking would be considered a practical and social endeavour. In fact, Burbules claims that the criteria for the adequacy of reasoning processes lie in the practical efficacy and social acceptability of the conclusion the processes derive; they are contextual, interactive and communicative.

The first feature looks promising for moral education, revealing the internal connection of critical thinking to moral education. But the second feature appears problematic for moral education. Burbules's pragmatic account of reasonableness underlying the second feature presupposes the postmodern proposition that the concept of rationality in itself is a socially constructed human invention. For Burbules, what prevents us from falling *entirely* into relativism is our reliance upon communicative and social interactions through which we judge the practical efficacy and social acceptability of our thoughts and actions. What is distinctive about this pragmatic response to moral difference is that the point for reasonable disagreement with others is *pragmatically* determined, pragmatic in the sense of driving the process of intellectual, moral and political development. But would pragmatic criteria in the face of moral disagreement end up leading us into the difficulties of relativism despite Burbules's claim to the contrary?

To admit *objectively* that the concept of (our) rationality is socially constructed is one thing, and to be committed *personally* to a particular concept of rationality as *my* or *our value* is another. This means that, even if we are aware that the concept of rationality, including ours, is historically contingent, this awareness does not make us immediately stop being committed to it by forcing us to take a relativist attitude. But it should not leave everything where it was either. How should this awareness affect us, then, in our ethical thinking? Although the pragmatic answer given by Burbules is one response to this question, I still find it unsatisfactory. What seems to be at stake in this question is not whether there is a way for us to avoid relativism altogether, which does not seem to be possible; it is rather how much room we can *coherently* find for thinking in a relativist way.

Williams (ibid., p. 160) holds that both the relativist, who thinks that the judgements of one group apply just to that group, and the other party, who thinks that any group's judgement must apply to everyone, are both wrong. According to him, if we are going to accommodate the relativists' concerns, we should not simply draw a line between ourselves and others. Rather, we should recognize that others are at varying distances from us, and we should also see that our reactions and relations to other groups are themselves part of our ethical life. I agree with his view as a realistic response to cultural pluralism. Yet we still feel that some disagreements and divergences are more important than others because we are concerned with the question of what life we are going to live as a group. I think this is the very moment when we feel forced to justify our moral outlook against others'. But what matters in this justification is not just to know how to accept the possibility of legitimate disagreement with others in moral arguments, but to know *in what spirit* to disagree rationally.

To make this point clearer, let me cite Stanley Cavell:

> But in the moral cases *what* is 'enough' is itself part of the content of the argument. What is enough to counter my claim to be right or justified in taking 'a certain' action is up to me, up to me to determine. ... I can *refuse to accept* a 'ground for doubt' (raised by others) without impugning it as false, and without supplying a new basis, and yet not automatically be dismissed as irrational or morally incompetent. What I *cannot* do, and yet maintain my position as morally competent, is to deny the *relevance* of your doubts, ... to fail to see that they require a determination by me. But in epistemological contexts, the relevance of the doubt is itself enough to impugn the basis as it stands, and therewith the claim to knowledge. (Cavell, 1979, p. 267)

Cavell suggests one way of understanding what it means for us to *disagree rationally* in moral arguments by describing the subtle characteristics of our moral agency in rationally disagreeing with others. Cavell seems to claim that what matters in moral arguments may not necessarily be to find out whether the position we take is rationally justified or not (or more or less reasonable), but to *come to know* where I stand in relation to the position I claim to take or how much I can take responsibility for the position I claim to take. Of course, I could assess, when confronted by others' questioning, the position I take to be flawed and decide to withdraw myself from that position. But this can be said to be part of the process through which I come to find out what position I really take and whether it is the one I can respect. And, in Cavell's view, in coming to know what my position is and how much I am willing to be committed to it, which can be brought about by serious discussion with others, the grounds for doubt about my own position become less important to me.

For Cavell, what is at stake in moral arguments is not exactly whether others know our world, but to what extent we care to *live in* the same moral universe. Thus, Cavell concludes that 'what is at stake ... is not validity of morality as a whole but the nature or quality of our relationship to one another' (ibid., p. 268). While refusing to accept the ground for doubt since my commitment to my value means so much to who I am, I do not need to take it as false since I cannot deny that it may be relevant to the epistemological status of my moral outlook. The extent of the room in which we can think in a relativist way may then be determined by the degree to which we care to live in the same moral universe as others. In this sense, for Cavell, our rational disagreement in moral arguments can be justified only for a *moral* reason.

Thus, this view can be said to imply that moral arguments in moral education are not to be directed to moral knowledge as rationally justifiable positions, but to *reflection* upon one's own moral position and one's relation to the position. But this reflection can be said to be the kind of reflection which demands that we suffer from doubt about the epistemic ground of our moral position in pursuit of truth, yet which still leaves us room for our will to take up the position as our own despite the uncertainty of the ground. This sort of reflection has potential for moral education in pluralist societies because it allows for the possibility of the ethical state where we can live in a non-relativist way with a relativist understanding of the world. Hence we may now formulate that the purpose of critical thinking in moral education is to cultivate in our students this sort of ethical state. Let me further develop this thesis.

Critical Thinking as Ethical Reflection

In moral education, the fostering of critical thinking is usually expected to lead students to struggle against the uncritical acceptance of the moral habits and opinions that have formed their character from early on in their childhood. That is, critical thinking can be described as a form of questioning their moral knowledge of what it is right to believe or do, the knowledge which they have relied on to find their way around the social world from their childhood. But, what purpose exactly is critical thinking supposed to serve in moral education? The purpose it may serve is to initiate reflection by asking the justificatory reason of the practice, so that students might imagine possibilities beyond their current set of commitments or moral beliefs. As a result, as I have shown with regard to Cavell's view, this reflection will allow them the possibility of autonomy in the sense that it enables them to *will for themselves* a commitment to ideas and beliefs *beyond rational justification*, even those handed down from their parents or teachers. However, would it be sufficient for moral education to facilitate students' *learned ownership* of those moral ideas and beliefs?

Given the nature of the contemporary world where a diversity of moral outlooks is unavoidable, this learned ownership of ours is accompanied by a consciousness of the non-objectivity of our own moral outlook. But, it seems that once we are *conscious* of the non-objectivity of it, it should affect the way in which we see the application of our moral outlook. According to Williams (ibid., p. 159), there are two mistaken, yet common, responses to this consciousness. One is that we think that this consciousness should just switch off our ethical reactions when we are confronted with an alternative outlook, believing that this consciousness of the non-objectivity of moral knowledge demands that we take a relativist view that requires us to be equally well disposed to everyone's moral beliefs. This is of course a confused response because it takes the non-objectivity of moral beliefs to 'issue in a non-relativist morality of universal tolerance'. It mistakenly takes up a universal morality, i.e. universal tolerance, when it denies such a thing. The other is that, despite a consciousness of the non-objectivity of moral beliefs, we can go on, simply saying that we are right and everyone else is wrong; we affirm our values and reject theirs on the non-objectivist view. Either way, such consciousness would just leave everything where it was and not affect our ethical thought, which is an inadequate as well as a dishonest response. So, how should the consciousness of non-objectivity affect our ethical thinking?

In posing and seeking an answer to this question, Williams (ibid., p. 112) distinguishes ethical reflection that leads to *theory* from ethical reflection that asks for an *explanation* of our motives, a psychological or social insight into our ethical practices. While the former seeks justificatory reasons for one's ethical practice, the latter pursues self-knowledge of it. For Williams, only the latter kind of ethical reflection goes beyond enabling students to have ownership of their moral ideas and beliefs. He characterizes the nature of ethical reflection in the latter sense as follows: before we reflect we could genuinely find our way around the social world by using our ethical knowledge of what it is right to believe or do; but once we reflect upon it, we feel that we should be doing something else. That is, the ethical reflection becomes part of the practice it considers and inherently modifies the ethical practice, even with our reassured commitment to it. In this sense, ethical reflection may destroy our ethical knowledge. But, according to Williams (ibid., p. 168), 'in the process of losing ethical knowledge we may gain knowledge of other kinds, about human nature, history, or what the world is actually like'; in other words, 'we can gain knowledge about, or around, the ethical'. Thus, Williams claims that 'inside the ethical, by the same process, we may gain *understanding*' (ibid.).[4]

Williams thus reformulates critical thinking suitable to ethical matters or moral education in terms of explanatory reflection rather than justificatory reasoning. To clarify the characteristics of this form of ethical reflection, we need to consider the meaning of *understanding* that this reflection pursues, as opposed to the knowledge that this reflection tends to destroy. Williams proposes that we should get our students to reflect on their individual or collective ethical practice. What does he mean by this? He recommends (ibid., p. 113) that we give up a linear model in giving reasons for all of our ethical practice. He even suggests that rationalizing as much as possible need not be understood as doing the next best thing, because this is to look at in the wrong direction. But he thinks that we might still be left with the possibility that for every practice there may be some reason, so that we might be able to show how a given practice hangs together with other practices in a way that makes social and psychological sense. But this means neither that we can meet a demand for justification made by someone standing outside our practices, nor that we will be able to justify them even to ourselves: the practices are so close to our own experiences that the reason we give will simply count as stronger than any reasons given by others for it.

Then why do we need to reflect on our ethical practice? According to Williams, the reflection would reveal the fact that certain practices or sentiments are not what they are taken to be, so as to lead us to understand the motive for our behaviour or the social roles involved; this reflection in itself will then be a part of our lives that can affect our practice one way or another. According to Williams, the ethical reflection should seek as much shared understanding on any given issue and use ethical materials that make sense in the context of reflective discussion. This differs from critical thinking that pursues theory or justificatory reasoning for general propositions or systemization. Here Williams makes it clear why critical thinking as justificatory reasoning cannot be adequate to ethical thinking. According to him (ibid., p. 116), people who practise discrimination tend not to admit that 'he is black' or 'she is a woman' is their reason: rationalization takes place with some reasons that better serve their purpose. Thus, rational argument against the injustice or cruelty or even inconsistency of their practice would hardly challenge them, since their beliefs are usually guarded against reflection because those beliefs suit the interests of the believers. Williams calls this irrationality in a deep form, and holds that this irrationality of beliefs, of self-deception, of social deceit cannot be exposed or cured by invoking critical thinking as justificatory reasoning, but by encouraging them to reflect on what they are doing.

Ethical reflection on our own practice does not merely require self-examination of our motives, but also needs to involve *theoretical* understanding of other kinds to be able to explain how and why a certain practice was derived, how it has shaped our experiences, and in what way our beliefs and desires are connected to it, as Williams (ibid.) notes. I think that this explanatory criticism would create in us a highly self-conscious awareness of what we are doing, including the consideration that we cannot be fully free from the practice. This awareness seems to be exactly what Williams refers to as the *understanding* of the ethical. Hence, we can conclude that ethical reflection in Williams's sense in moral education can bring to our students the learned ownership of their moral beliefs along with a broader understanding of their ethical practice based upon them—namely, the possibilities and limitations of the practice.

What is so useful about this notion of understanding for moral education is that it can help our students to avoid moral relativism despite their realization of the non-objectivity of their moral outlook by providing them with 'knowledge about human nature, history, or what the world is actually like' in relation to their ethical practice. Williams (ibid., p. 170) reminds us that our students' decisions to will for themselves their own moral outlook is not in a form of conviction based on the certainty of knowledge, but in a form of *confidence* based on social confirmation and support as well as rational argument. Thus, what matters now in our educators' consideration of moral education is narrowed down to two questions. One is: What kinds of institutions, upbringing, and public discourse would help foster our students' confidence in finding life worth living? The other is: What, from the perspective of the ethical life we actually have, do we count as a life worth living?

Notes

1. See the three essays on rationality and reason in *Critical Conversations in Philosophy of Education* (1995), edited by Wendy Kohli.
2. Here I use the terms 'moral' and 'ethical' interchangeably, taking them in a broad sense that includes obligations and duties as well as virtues.
3. In Siegel's formulation of critical thinking, the conceptual connection between epistemic virtue and moral virtue is not clear; it may probably simply be assumed.
4. According to Williams, Socrates made two assumptions that Williams himself does not accept. One is that Socrates thought it impossible that reflection should destroy knowledge since nothing unreflective could be knowledge in the first place. The other is that Socrates believed

that reflection led to knowledge and that knowledge was what matters. Williams rejects both of these assumptions for the following reasons. In the case of moral knowledge, knowledge without reflection is better in enabling us to go about the social world. On the other hand, ethical knowledge, though there is such a thing, is not necessarily the best ethical state. In morality, moral action should be considered prior to moral knowledge (Williams, 1985, p. 168).

References

Bailin, S. & Siegel, H. (2003) Critical Thinking, in: N. Blake, P. Smeyers, R. Smith, and P. Standish (eds), *The Blackwell Guide to the Philosophy of Education* (Oxford, Blackwell).

Blake, N., Smeyers, P., Smith, R. & Standish, P. (2003) *Philosophy of Education* (Oxford, Blackwell).

Bubules, N. (1995) Reasonable Doubt, in: W. Kohli (ed.), *Critical Conversations in Philosophy of Education* (New York, Routledge) ch. 7.

Cavell, S. (1979) *The Claim of Reason: Wittgenstein, skepticism, morality, and tragedy* (Oxford, Oxford University Press).

Kohli, W. (ed.) (1995) *Critical Conversations in Philosophy of Education* (New York, Routledge).

Plato (1981) *Five Dialogues*, trans. G. M. A. Grube (Indianapolis, Hackett Publishing).

Siegel, H. (1988) *Educating Reason: Rationality, critical thinking and education* (New York, Routledge).

Williams, B. (1985) *Ethics and the Limits of Philosophy* (Cambridge, MA, Harvard University Press).

Index

Note: 'n' after a page number refers to a note on that page.